Angelic Dialogues

by
Stephen R. Schwartz

RIVERRUN PRESS
Piermont, New York

For more information on books and recordings, and
further writings of
STEPHEN ROBBINS SCHWARTZ
please see the website:
compassionateselfcare.wordpress.com
or contact his widow, Donna, at
dtotten@whidbey.com

Cover art by Debra Koff Chapin using a process she originated called Touch Drawing.
Typesetting by Synergistic Data Systems
Book Design by Donna Schwartz
Printed in the United States of America

No part of this book may be used or reproduced in any manner whatsoever without written permission except for brief quotations for review purposes.

Copyright © 1993 by Riverrun Press.
All rights reserved.

ISBN: 0-936415-11-8

Contents

Forward i

1 1
Compassionate Self-Care and Angelic Dialogues

2 11
The space we fall into as the thought structure is transcended is warm and fulfilling all by itself.

3 21
So there you are with yourself in a tight, lonely space beating up the one who is in pain.

4 33
There is nothing you can tell yourself about pain that will heal it.

5 49
Our hurt becomes a door into a different kind of reality.

6 85
We have become so intermingled, so shared, that the "I love you" or "You love me" doesn't make sense. We share a unified field which is recognized to be love.

7 101
A deep relationship with someone else is impossible as long as we are terrified of ourselves.

8 115
Why would we deliberately choose to know nothing, to long for love honestly, and to confess our neediness?

9 133
We can use content to transcend content.

10 209
When the mind is clear, it is experienced as space.

11 227
The spiritual path is not a series of cathartic experiences; it is a movement toward deep trust and patient, attentive waiting.

FOREWORD

I have known, and loved, Stephen these past five years. His death in March, 1993, shortly after the completion of this book, greatly saddened me. It also has moved me—as well as others whom he has inspired—to continue to make his work available.

I came to Stephen's work from a background in scientific psychology, moderated by Jewish humanism and by the practice of psychotherapy oriented around Focusing (as developed by Eugene Gendlin, Ph.D.). When I met Stephen, I had been a clinical psychologist for about thirty-five years, primarily involved in private practice but also in educating psychology interns and psychiatry residents (currently with the Department of Psychiatry of the University of Washington). After five years of participating in workshops and personal dialogues with Stephen as well as listening to many of his audiotapes, I am not the same person I was. I was totally unprepared for the revolution which has happened for me—both in how I experience my personal life and what I know to be professionally possible. I have come to realize that Stephen's work represents a profound contribution to our understanding of what it means to be a human being and what it means to be truly helpful to another human being.

I often wondered what inhered in Stephen's work that led to such remarkable changes in how people experience themselves and their lives. For me, the result has been a greater ease, richer relationships and a much deepened sense of life's meaning. I have observed similarly far-reaching effects for many others who participated in workshops with Stephen or who read his books and listened to his recorded material. This has led me to wonder why, by contrast with Stephen's work, some of the typical ways in which people undertake to deal with life's pain—particularly psychotherapy—often seem to yield such pallid or unreliable benefits.

It is impossible to put into words the actual experience of the work Stephen called Compassionate Self-Care. Over the

i

years, my wife and friends have likened my efforts to conceptualize Stephen's work to the incongruity of trying to conceptualize music. As with music, Compassionate Self-Care derives its meaning from experiencing it. Nevertheless, I would like to share some of the experiences and understandings that have emerged from my personal journey with Stephen.

My first awareness in coming to Stephen's work was of a dissonance with the usual thrust of psychotherapy, which is to produce change. By contrast, Stephen never seemed interested in trying to "fix" anything or to "get" anywhere in his dialogic interactions. In working with people on issues ranging from AIDS to everyday relationship problems, Stephen seemed to come from the understanding that he was there to "join," to connect somehow, with the person. I was particularly baffled because Stephen was not undertaking to "form a relationship" in the typical psychological sense; that is, to provide a helpful milieu in which one psychotherapeutic technique or another could then be employed in the service of some eventual psychotherapeutic goal. Rather, the feeling of relationship was there to be experienced for its inherent value, a respectful noticing of intimacy and the distance from it. But why, I continued to wonder, was Stephen so interested in how two people were connecting to one another when there was work to be done on life problems?

Perhaps, among other things, connecting with someone allows the person access to what is actually going on in their direct experience of themselves. By way of illustration, in my early dialogues with Stephen there was a contrast between my approach to our exchanges and Stephen's approach. Typically, *my* interest was in trying to "solve" some issue in my life, whereas *his* interest always seemed to be greater clarification. His way of being with me never implied that the purpose of our exploring was to determine what was "wrong," thus requiring change or even help. Accordingly, I could then experience the subtleties of my inner life as they emerged from their embeddedness in automatic ways of responding. What I came to experience were "knowings," arising organically, rather than something I merely thought or speculated about.

I saw that I would enter a dialogue with Stephen by highlighting some feeling of distress or problematic issue in my life. This scenario seemed to have three main ingredients: the way I saw or construed the problem, the felt distress itself and the more or less urgent search for some way to bring about change. In order to effect change, I might seek some new understanding or perhaps a deeper underlying meaning or perhaps some whole new approach to it all—anything that would let me exercise a kind of executive control that I implicitly assumed I could have over the distress, if I could but find the "right way." However, I came to see that I had been finding one "right way" after another over many years; that there were hopeful new approaches which had manifested at different times, although each one eventually failed to bring about durable change. The same anxiety or fear or way of characterizing my "problem" continued to harass me, often in a slightly different guise. At that point, what struck me was the ludicrous futility of the whole change enterprise. The understanding emerged that it was the very judgment that there was something wrong—which, of course, would then require "fixing"—that actually created and perpetuated the "problem." The manner in which my mind had constructed the presumed fact of a problem *was* the problem.

By contrast, Stephen would ask me to notice my body, thus making it possible for me to witness the fact that all my efforts to change did have at least one highly interesting consequence: they did seem to create a congested, tense, or otherwise uncomfortable bodily feeling. Stephen often has described his work as involving *ahimsa*, or non-violence. It was remarkable to me to discover the violence I had been doing to myself in trying to change.

If we are not seeking change, we are left with coming to our feelings. This, of course, is easier said than done—partly because the pain often seems too great. But it is also, in part, because of the great confusion that exists for most people about the realm of feeling. A major part of the confusion seems to center around that part of our feeling life that we commonly call "emotions." Stephen's non-pressured exploration enables us to clarify the nature of the actual experience we designate as emotional—pain and all. In so doing, we become aware that previously our attention has been focused on our *interpretation* of the experience rather than on the experience itself.

Most people assume that emotions are located in some vague bodily space, or perhaps in the head, rather than physically in a specific location in the body. This obviously contributes to confusion. The direct experience of what we call an emotion is further obscured by the commentary or explanation about its presumed cause. Often this attribution of causality is so glued to the body discomfort that they seem to be the same thing. For example, I might feel a discomfort which I call fear or anxiety or sadness or despair. This is felt in some vague bodily way and is presumed to be about either an external cause (perhaps no intimacy in my life) or an internal cause (perhaps an inclination to treat myself with disrespect).

Stephen's effort is to come respectfully and with caring presence to the direct experience of what we refer to as the emotion. He invites us to note the obsessive focus on what we believe to be the cause of the emotion, and then to place our attention on the front of our body—particularly the neck, heart and solar plexus areas—which he refers to as the frontal membrane. He suggests that we notice the actual energy movements as they are occurring in the body.

With this change of attention, we permit ourselves to experience no longer being in the throes of continually repeating the storyline of the emotion—and thus, momentarily, to step out of the prison of the past. At the same time, as we come to the bodily experience itself, we begin to notice that the "bad" emotion is constricted energy—typically a tension, congestion or heaviness. This was enormously relieving to me—to find that the bogeyman of emotions with which I had wrestled for many years might consist of bodily sensations. It was as if a demon had just disappeared! In contrast to the frustrations that had accrued through my years of struggles to get rid of the emotions, it now seemed possible, and even interesting, to explore the actual physical feeling experience.

How lovely it was, in coming to myself with Compassionate Self-Care, either alone or in dialogue with Stephen, not to have to struggle with beliefs about my life or judgments about my feelings. And if such beliefs and judgments did arise, how lovely not to struggle with even the tension they evoked. Instead, I could just notice my way of being in the world and breathe easily with whatever bodily experience I was having. This, of course, is not how I am always able to come to my experience; it is rather a practice to be gently pursued.

Although there is never a push or coercion to change in any way, ironically enough it is from this accepting place that change can occur. It has been astounding to me to discover, as one example of my own change of consciousness, that I no longer have to wrestle with an almost life-long feeling of anxiety. Most mornings of my life since starting grade school, I awoke with an emotion I labeled fear or anxiety. Especially in my adult life, I worked for extended periods of time to be rid of it—through classical treatment modalities such as psychoanalysis and with many self-help strategies—all to no avail. The anxiety maintained itself and I grew more frustrated and despairing of change. As a result of my experience with Compassionate Self-Care, I find that I no longer experience the morning anxiety. I didn't do anything; I have no sense of having brought about the change. It is just something that I no longer experience.

What happened to the emotion I called fear or anxiety? I have found that by being present with the physical sensations in my body rather than struggling against feelings I regard as unacceptable, my "problems" begin to take on another complexion and even dissipate. One of the profound awarenesses arising from the orientation of Compassionate Self-Care may then be available to be experienced—the coursing of life energy in the bodily frame in a way unique to that person, at that time. We may even feel more warmth and a greater sense of relatedness. The ecological truth of our bodily participation in universal life energy is experienced as the healing process is engaged in the body. (By contrast, the thrust of much of contemporary psychotherapy is to change beliefs. One wonders how illusory it is to think that such mind-engineering can be effected, especially in the case of deeply-held, probably bodily-organized habits of belief.)

I also have been struck by the meeting of East and West in Stephen's work. One can notice interesting parallels between what people experience in the dialogues that follow in this book and what is often reported by experienced meditators. I am aware of many reports by long-term meditators of their experience of the prison of the mind. In Compassionate Self-Care, as well as in meditation, a deep awareness can emerge of the conditioned mind's sway over our lives and the creation thereby of many of the problems of our lives. Furthermore, in meditative traditions such as Vipassana, Zen and others, the emotional life of the person comes into relief and bodily energies are experienced, not unlike what I have described as inherent in Stephen's work.

I believe that Stephen's work represents a unique development in our capacity to enable human awareness and understanding; in short, to "know oneself." My impression is that we have labored with the approach of psychology which, over the last hundred years or so, has sought to understand a person by studying him or her objectively; in effect, by setting the person at a distance, and then thinking about the meaning of various aspects of behavior. By contrast, the meditative traditions recognize that knowing our actual depth of being can come only through direct experience, and never through any theory *about* one's inner experience. Accordingly, the great wisdom arising from meditation has come as a result of the practice of *presence* with one's actual experience of being. One of Stephen's notable achievements in what he calls "angelic dialogues" is to have adapted the practice of presence to the *interactive space*. This contrasts with the traditional meditative way of engaging in more solitary and non-verbal practice. Stephen offers in the angelic dialogues in this book the practice of presence in warm, respectful relationship as a means of intentionally experiencing inner reality.

Stephen's orientation also contrasts with the psychological approach, particularly in that he is suggesting *direct participation* in our experience of ourselves rather than *thinking about* our experience. Thus, it is by participative engagement with our pain and our problems that he invites us to walk the path of self-knowing. And it is by not making our survival modes and our pain into problems, but instead by attending to how we are physically experiencing them in our bodies, that we can facilitate an evolutionary path in our own lives. In an October, 1992, interview in *The Sun* magazine, Stephen explains: "In self-care work, the emphasis is on using the problem and the pain as a bridge between the tight place we find ourselves caught in and spaciousness itself. In this work, the mental struggle is not ignored....We come back to the body, feel the body, attend to the body and alternately speak about the problem, even in great detail." He emphasizes that this is not in order "to gain an insight which will allow us to see the problem." It is rather that by attending to the body in the context just alluded to, what is facilitated is "dropping out of the problem altogether and merging into the natural spaciousness that exists in and around the body."

Stephen thus calls attention to an expanded awareness of the nature of the body, an awareness that can be facilitated by the deep exploration of interactive space portrayed in *Angelic Dialogues*. He contrasts this deeper understanding of the body with our normal everyday perception of the body as a density. Stephen writes: "We honor the body because it is more than what it looks like. This body is not simply the physical appearance that we can see and touch. Within the body and surrounding it, there is an energetic field which cannot usually be seen by the naked eye. The visible body is like the hub of a wheel. From its core there are spokes which extend in every direction. These spokes are a shimmering illumination, an invisible radiance." It is this energetic understanding—in Compassionate Self-Care practice, either with oneself or in dialogue—which may point the way to both a refined experience of relationship and a further path out of the prison of our minds and our emotions.

While the energetic phenomena referred to above may not yet have been scientifically established, Stephen calls our attention to the essential fact that its effects can be felt. (I might note here that an energetic field such as that alluded to by Stephen seems, to me, to be implicit in the understandings of quantum physics. Also, the effects of these energetic phenomena on human interactions are now being actively explored as evidenced by the papers and research presented at conferences sponsored by the International Society for the Study of Subtle Energies and Energy Medicine.)

To follow Stephen's remarkable understanding of this energetic context, we need to note his emphasis, time and again, that relationship (true connection) is a bodily phenomenon—my body, energetically, with your body. Our bodies are not merely containers for the purpose of carrying around heads with thoughts—thoughts to be exchanged from one container to another. Rather, we are bodies relating to other bodies through energies which can be felt, but which we are largely unaware of feeling because we focus so much of our attention on our thoughts, beliefs, and judgments. In contrast to merely exchanging thoughts, even highly personal thoughts, we can actually feel energies of engagement and holdbacks to engagement. In this way, it seems to me, our Western understanding of what is possible for human beings is expanded; that is, we can directly experience the realm of relationship which Martin Buber has so eloquently written about as the "between."

Finally, I would like to consider why Stephen refers to these dialogues as "angelic." Stephen suggests that "angelic" may be taken to designate dialogue which attends to body feelings, since that is "a way for many to find the next step in their lives and to embrace the great mystery which guides us all." He also notes that such dialogues "offer, in the gentlest way, a chance to pray through the body and to receive a vision of our life from a perspective which is not bound by the restraints of the past." Angelic is not a word I would dare to use—but it seems appropriate, indeed natural, for Stephen. For my own understanding, I note that the etymology of angel connotes "emissary," "message bearer." I take this to refer to the difference between casual conversation, where information may be exchanged, and the presence of an emissary in an angelic dialogue, bearing a message of a more universal (energetic, perhaps divine) nature. Perhaps the message is that our culture's fixation on psychological meaning and even on spiritual "understanding" is selling us short. Perhaps we can allow ourselves greater expectations. As creatures of the universe, not merely reasoning beings, we may aspire to healing through connection—with ourselves and with others through Compassionate Self-Care.

Arnold Katz, Ph.D.

Angelic Dialogues

1

Compassionate Self-Care and Angelic Dialogues

Compassionate Self-Care is not about subduing or controlling the mind. This work involves a simple release of the attention from thought so that it can rest with the portal of the heart, the breath and with the body in a more general way. We do not fight the mind. We simply shift our attention to the breath, participating in the gentle rhythmic movements of the body as it inhales and exhales. In so doing we allow our feelings to exist in a simple, physical way. This innocent movement of the attention from thinking to the heart creates an opportunity to discover, even briefly, a dimension of life which is different from that unruly force we call the mind. We pull the sash and view something which has been hidden from us for a long time. Maybe we weren't even sure it was there. But it is. Such an assurance has been given throughout time. A realm exists on the other side of the illusions and delusions of the mind. That realm becomes available when we open to ourselves in such a way that a hidden passage gets cleared. We become gently aware of a dimension which is filled with the possibility of adventure and discovery.

We stay with the body and the breath. We allow the rhythm of the breathing to exist in an uninterrupted way. Whatever we feel in the body is okay. We don't prod or try to make it go away. We let the body settle down and drift away from its habitual defense.

If the mind begins to repeat its worn-out view of things, we notice that in an open way and then return our attention to the breath. We leave the thoughts behind. If a particular strand of thought persists, the chances are that a corresponding intensity exists in the body — a hurt, a raw place, a woundedness that needs our care.

Underneath all our obsessions, riding just beneath the surface, but obscured by a fixation on content, something hurts in the body. The body attempts to defend itself against that hurt and tenses. As it does so, the mind's demands are amplified. But underneath the tension, and transcending the mind's demands, we can find an ache, an innocent longing for something other than our current reality frame. We turn to the longing and wait. We consciously participate in our longing.

What we see around us, our picture of reality, is made up of certain perceptual constraints which arise from the past. This perception does not represent an objective fact or an accurate picture of the whole. It is only a fragment of what exists, a tiny thread of limited possibilities.

There is more to life than what we currently perceive, more than what we are currently taking in. Each of us longs to step outside the conditions of our existence and to experience the greater arena, the deeper understanding. We know intuitively that something else exists.

There is something that we want, but it is not always clear what it is or how to get it. Something elusive beckons and sometimes its call seems very real. But there are times when we feel caught inside a prison of our own making and don't know how to bring the walls down. We long for a reality which is greater than the one we have assumed to be true.

Each of us has experienced at one time or another, a vague frustration with the situation at hand, a hunger for the next step. We want to know something more about our lives than what thoughts invent, but it feels like we are being held back. Two forces live within, a longing to expand and a holdback. They press against each other, they struggle. And this struggle is often dramatized in our relationships to each other, to money, to our past and to our dreams for the future. We long for greatness, but feel held back in various ways.

The longing and the struggle with it has led to a search, a desire for answers. We look for some insight, idea or philosophical construct which will release us from our belief in limits and our longing for something else. There are times when we treat our longing with disrespect, when we fight with it, hate it and even try to push it away. There are times when our longing confuses us and times when we know we must wait.

It is certainly possible to perceive the interplay between the longing and the restraint as a problem or even as a kind of failure. Yet, from another vantage point, this same interplay can become the most important internal event we might face as human beings. This simple interaction between a sense of limitations and the desire for something greater is the passkey for the journey ahead. It represents the next step for each of us.

Angelic Dialogues offer a path toward a new relationship to ourselves in which we honor our frustration by understanding it on a new level. Human beings long to experience the mystery of existence in an open way, to be fed by love and to express freely. But there is also a block. We must learn how to honor the longing and the block as well. In so doing, a guiding wisdom can be uncovered, a clear indication of the next step.

When we compassionately observe ourselves, breathing and being with the feelings, we might notice that there is a part of us which would like to be taken care of. There is a part of us which would like to have a big brother or sister who knows something we do not know, who would give hints and indications about what to do next, but would not inflict their judgments and advice. We would all like to be given some delicate instructions about what decisions to make, what path to follow and how to work creatively and peacefully with the circumstances we must face. Conscious knowledge is so limited.

Each of us longs to expand and each of us is blocked. The endless refrains of thought distract us from both the longing and the block. We have made something up about what our conflict means and have become absorbed in a debate which has no grounded bearing on the situation as it exists. Inside, somewhere, we are aware that trying to figure out what to do next, what steps to take, is mostly futile because the future is an unknown. The effects of our decisions can't be understood in advance. We have a natural desire to be lovingly guided, gently pushed in a particular direction so that our lives can be fresh and not merely a reiteration of the past.

Inside is a longing. It has been there for a long, long time. And if we are clear with ourselves, we can see how this longing has motivated many of our responses to life's events. We haven't always approached it in an honest way. There are times when we have tried to distract ourselves from the longing and times when we have tried to suppress it. There are times when we have assumed that someone, something, some event or achievement would satisfy it. We have embraced that person or thing for a while, felt thrilled and filled with hopefulness, and then realized that our embrace did not bring an end to our desiring. More lay underneath.

At times we have judged our longing as the worst part of ourselves, that which is always out of peace. Sometimes, however, we are intrigued and fascinated by it because within lies a hint of something else, something more, something greater, something just over the edge of our current perception — more magnetic than the ho-hum of everyday routines.

Our longing is often perceived as an enemy and only sometimes as a friend. It inevitably reminds us that there is more to life than our current perception lets in. We want to step outside of boundaries, but we are cautious, tentative and even a little afraid.

It may seem sometimes as if an unseen obstacle is holding us back. We perceive ourselves to be caught in an invisible trap, knowing vaguely what we want, but not knowing how to attain it. This sense of entrapment may not seem severe, but there are times when it appears stark and all too clear. We are caught in a cage, shaking the bars and knocking on the gate. Sometimes we can hear something knocking back, calling our name, but more often, we can't. What is the key? Who can show the way?

As human beings we are urged toward the infinite. When this urge is felt, it can be interpreted in many different ways. We might see it as a neurosis, a weakness, an issue or as a psychological dilemma in need of insight or analysis. Sometimes we seek to blame. But our urge is not a weakness, an issue or problem. It is our dignity and true strength. It is the path out of our apparent trap. It is the way.

Anyone who is attracted to spirituality senses that life holds more than the phenomena which we perceive through our five senses. Life is more than a random series of events which please or displease according to how much pleasure or pain they bring. Those who are attracted to a spiritual quest intuit that life can offer more than what we currently perceive. We have begun to acknowledge our hunger.

Compassionate Self-Care is a path which allows us to be so respectful of our longing that we recognize it to be a spontaneous and natural prayer. We don't want to feel vacant, empty, alone or imprisoned by a code of reality which the mind invents. We want freedom and guidance as well. We want to follow the call.

One of the principles of Compassionate Self-Care is that the body is an opening, a way to union even though we may perceive it to be an enclosure, a little fortress with some awareness inside. The body is a passageway, an entry into a cathedral. It is the door to spaciousness. When we become aware of the body in this way, we begin to experience life differently and might even feel the presence of invisible forces, wisdom bearers, that can give strength, compassion and understanding to us in our everyday affairs.

The path of Compassionate Self-Care reveals that true wisdom is not a mental experience. It is not a function of thought. Wisdom is a heart experience, a bodily phenomenon. If we are to find guidance in this life, to enter into communion with subtle realms and find the Presence of Love, it will be necessary to transcend the ordinary mechanisms of thought and discover something new about the body. The body is a passageway to space from space. It is not evidence of our isolation or separation from the whole. It is instead an integral part of things seen and unseen.

This earth is not the only arena of consciousness in the universe. What we call reality is just one piece of an enormous and mysterious whole. Layered into our so-called reality are many other dimensions which can not easily be seen. Certain individuals throughout time have peeled away the veil of sensory perception and have witnessed the life beyond. Some have shared their experiences and have told of presences, beings, forces, which guide and assist the destiny of humankind. We are not alone, but our sense of aloneness holds the key to reunion and communion with all that is.

Those who have come to the edge of life, who have passed through the veil and then returned, indicate that there are Beings who guide us. They don't necessarily intervene in our affairs, fixing circumstances and making things right, but they do offer compassion, guidance and deep care. We must turn to them in a conscious way before they can become fully active on our behalf.

The human body is an unbelievably subtle and complex phenomenon. It is not a device which carries around a head. It constantly receives something of vast importance to us and gives back something of importance to the universe itself. Unseen energies come to the body and are taken into it. They vibrate in a particular way, creating a felt tone. We may experience that tone, but interpret it as something personal — as an emotion, perhaps.

Our feelings are messages. They are transmissions. They do not mean what we think they do. In order to hear the message of our feelings, we must reorient the way we react to them by listening differently. We must learn how to turn toward the tone of a feeling, instead of to our ideas about it. We must learn to accept the sacred nature of our experience and to take in the wisdom and nourishment it brings.

The mind is obsessed by information, yet it doesn't know how to deal with all the information it has. It can't make sense out of all the pieces. Every feeling is a many-layered communication which contains the wisdom of the whole. Feelings are not pieces of information. When we turn our attention to the heart, we can discover the evolutionary message which resonates there and is often interpreted as an emotion.

We don't have to live as if the body were a jail cell. It is not a density, but only appears that way due to our current perception of it. The body is a visible tone. It is an opening, an invitation, a constant possibility. It is not the beginning and end of our existence. It is only one phase of it.

Finding guidance, touching the deeper realities of life, involve unlearning what we think our feelings mean and allowing ourselves to be with them at the physical level alone. We give ourselves permission to feel our longing without making any demand upon it at all.

The dialogues, which have always been an integral part of the Compassionate Self-Care work, are called Angelic Dialogues because they help us to give up the barren and often self-destructive labels that have become attached to our feelings and our life circumstances. They also offer, in the gentlest way, a chance to pray through the body and to receive a vision of our life from a perspective which is not bound by the restraints of the past. It has been a way for many to find the next step in their lives and to embrace the great mystery which guides us all.

Over the years people have gathered to explore their lives from a radically different perspective. Angelic Dialogues is not a discussion of psychological insights or the communication of abstract ideas. It is instead a way to remove the thorny crown of self-hate and to honor our lives as they are, so that a creative force can begin to consciously come through us.

Angelic Dialogues and Compassionate Self-Care are not programs which attempt to show us how to fix ourselves, get better or to find what we are missing. They are instead ways of translating everything we have judged to be wrong or weak about ourselves into a fiery force of love and understanding.

Angelic Dialogues take place in the warm sphere of relationship as a result of a unified prayer, a conscious opening. They are participatory explorations in self-respect and creative responses to the mystery of this life.

During a group session, what is discussed with one person is unique to that person on the level of content, but is deeply enriching and transforming to all who sit and participate, silently or otherwise. We feel ourselves as one being, able to recall something ancient, sacred and beautiful about ourselves and each other.

Angelic Dialogues leave no one out, but at the same time, no one is ever pushed to get anywhere, to be anything, to overcome something or to see life in a particular way. It could not be any other way. We sit together in the prayer of no regrets, respecting ourselves and each other in just the way an angel might.

Compassionate Self-Care and Angelic Dialogues represent an invitation to explore something which is often ignored — our dignity, our deep connection to each other and a direct experience of self-love.

2

The space we fall into as
the thought structure is transcended
is warm and fulfilling
all by itself.

Dale: There is an experience going on which at this point in my life is causing me some pain. I want to talk about it in terms of what we have been looking at here.

I keep focusing on wanting to have a relationship with somebody and putting myself kind of on the back burner. Sometimes the desire manifests itself as wanting an actual relationship and sometimes it manifests as wanting a sexual relationship only.

I am at the point of being able to let go and I feel like I keep wanting to say to myself that the only person I need to have a relationship with right now is God. That usually works, except then I get really anxious about when will God provide me with the kind of personal relationship that I want.

I think I already understand my situation in certain ways but I want to open it up and see if you could shed some light on it in a way that is healing so that when I am alone, I feel more complete.

Are you saying to me that when you are alone you don't feel complete? I just want to be sure that I understood the last statement you made.

Dale: Yes, I feel like I am not enough when I'm alone and I feel very needy in that way.

In order to understand what you are saying, it is very important that we enter into a refined and delicate communication. If you don't mind, I need to ask you a question or two and then let's see if we can unstrand the threads of what you are going through.

When you say that you feel incomplete, how does that feel? How do you know you are feeling incomplete? I don't understand what it means to feel incomplete. Can you try to express that to me?

Dale: It feels uncomfortable. It's like not having or feeling enough love for myself.

When you say, "I don't feel that I have enough love for myself"—just so that you and I are very clear—is that a thought or a feeling?

Dale: It is probably more a thought.

There is a thought there. In other words, something is being explained by that thought. Now when we speak of the feeling, where do you experience it? How do you know you are having a feeling and not a thought?

Dale: Discomfort.

The discomfort is where?

Dale: It feels....it feels alone. I feel....

Okay, I understand what you are saying, and forgive me for prodding, but it is the only way we can really understand. When I hear you say, "It feels alone," I don't know what you mean. I am not clear and I want to be very clear with you.

Dale: I understand. It feels like....anxious.

Okay, and the anxiety is where?

Dale: It ends up surrounding my chest, not knowing what to do....

But the "not knowing what to do" is different from that which is surrounding your chest, isn't that true?

Dale: Yes.

I mean the "not knowing what to do" is a specific kind of thought pattern. That which is surrounding your chest really doesn't have a "do" or a "not do" attached to it. It is an experience in and of itself.

The "not knowing what to do" is a relationship to a particular feeling experience. It functions as a habit. "When I feel this sensation, then I have a particular stream of thoughts about not knowing what to do." An association has been made between a certain bodily experience and a cluster of thoughts. This is conditioning. The two seem to emerge simultaneously, but they are actually different. Do you follow what I am saying here?

Dale: Yes.

The anxiety—what you are calling anxiety—is not confusion; it is something else. The confusion is on the level of thought.

Dale: Yes.

So in order for you and me to really understand what it is we are talking about, it may be necessary to free the bodily side of your experience from the word "anxiety" or the thought, "I don't know what to do."

Here, we don't want to define your feelings in a way that is pat, easy and trivial. We want to know you and to feel you as a uniqueness, but to do that we must come into the uniqueness of your experience. We don't even know what anxiety is. All we know is that you are having an experience at the physical level and that you can locate it somewhere in and around the chest. Are you feeling it right now? Is it there in a strong way?

Dale: No, right now I am feeling very supported.

Very supported. And how do you know you're feeling that?

Dale: I feel warm.

Do you feel warm in the same physical location that you were feeling the anxiety?

Dale: Yes.

In other words the problem doesn't exist right now.

Dale: I can feel it slightly, but there is real warmth right now. I feel cared for.

So in this present moment, as you and I sit together, there is no problem.

Dale: Right.

And you feel warm and cared for. Let's go to that together for just a minute. Let's actually share that. This is the experience of not having a problem. "I feel warm." And that warmth is a living experience, not a thought. It's a warmth in the body. Do you feel confused at this moment?

Dale: Not right now, no.

So as you sit here, even the confusion is gone.

Dale: I feel a little light-headed, but not confused.

Now when you brought up the problem, you brought it up in terms of something that kind of menaces you "out there," but it isn't menacing you right here, now.

Dale: Right.

So we are speaking about something that you anticipate is going to happen in the future because it has happened to you so many times in the past.

Dale: Yes.

But you weren't speaking about what is actually here with you at this moment. The observation we can make, which is a beautiful observation, is that the warmth —and correct me if I am wrong — and what you were calling the anxiety, take place in the same physical space.

Dale: Yes.

Now this could lead to one of two conclusions: a) the warmth and the anxiety are different and, when the warmth is there, it is there because, in some way, it has pushed the anxiety away, and the anxiety is there because it has pushed the warmth away; or b) they are differing versions of the same experience.

Dale: Yeah, sometimes recently I have come to feel that they are different versions of the same feelings. When I ran away, it became aloneness; otherwise it was very different. I really saw that.

Now it's interesting that when you call it aloneness and you run away from it, there is only one place to run to — into thoughts where the feeling doesn't seem to exist. When you run away, the earmark of your running is, "I don't know what to do."

Dale: And then I practice certain behaviors that sort of push the feeling more into the background. The thoughts get stronger.

Exactly. The cycle that you go through is an attempt to make foreign and push away that which you think you don't want to experience directly. Now, that's aloneness. That's a certified lonely experience —to have something going on in the body which we feel we don't want to have going on there and then to push our attention into thought and fantasy so that we stay distracted from our own body.

The thinking mechanism suggests that the feeling is about something you do in relationship, or the need for relationship, or a problem that you have. Thinking is describing it for you. But when you allow yourself, as you have done tonight, to simply come to the present, to the bodily present, you discover that you feel warmth.

Dale: Just sitting with it and allowing it to be there and being surrounded by others and sharing it feels warm.

Yes, this warmth is something that feels related, doesn't it? The warmth that you're feeling now is a connection between you and me as well as a connection with the others who are here. The warmth is not loneliness.

Dale: It's fullness.

It's fullness and so you don't feel incomplete as you sit here right now. This is not a facetious question; it is a genuine question, and it's an important one although it may have a certain humor to it: What is the problem? I don't remember anymore what your problem was. Do you?

Dale: No.

I mean, is that true? In order to come back to the problem would you have to manufacture it?

Dale: I would have to make it up again.

You would have to make it up again. That's an interesting statement and a very important one. In order to experience the problem, you would have to make it up again. Now we are in a radical and delicate place — a place I know that could, on the one hand, scare someone off, or be strangely confusing to the intellect. All we're saying, however, is that as you sit here without the vehicle of thought, turned toward yourself in a direct and respecting manner, you discover that the problem was made up. I don't want to put words in your mouth. I want to be sure that this is what you are observing.

Dale: Yes, this is something that I pretty much knew.

That the whole configuration of insights and analysis, difficulties and disturbances, in relationship to this particular experience, were all fabricated. The truth is that certain movements of energy are occurring in the body and they are neither confusing nor not confusing. They are what they are. And when you allow yourself, in a sensitive and simple way, to experience what's going on, the problem disappears.

Dale: Yeah, I don't have to tell myself a story about it.

Right, there's nothing.

Dale: There's just experiencing the feeling.

Yes, this is self-care. You don't attend to the conflict. You attend to the heart, the area around the heart and the body, in a more general way. We are delicate beings, dwelling in a mysterious place, and we experience waves of energy in the body. Period. We have given the thought process a kind of permission to exploit those waves for purposes which are not entirely clear.

When that which is exploiting the feeling is no longer given permission to do so, the problem, as we knew it, disappears and something else appears which feels cared for, alive, warm and connected.

Dale: Yeah, it helps. I've heard you refer to the body before as a holy vessel, and that Spirit is the essence which fills that vessel.

Spirit can be felt as waves of feeling. When we name those feelings in demeaning ways, we find ourselves caught in chains. When we allow those feelings to remain unnamed, they pulsate in the body. Our feelings are waves of love being experienced in a variety of ways.

When a person is able to release themselves from patterns of demeaning thought and to find the energetic wave at the source of all so-called emotional experiences, we have the opportunity to create in free and uncluttered ways. When we are manacled by thought, caught in the clutches of old beliefs, we are merely repeating some teaching that we took on in the past.

Coming to the present and recognizing the warmth which is there evokes the possibility of a true creative act. We can begin to use both body and mind differently. The impulse of life, which we had burdened with our personalized concerns now becomes an available creative force. This is the power of coming to the space in which the past no longer exists. It no longer defines our current experiences.

The space which we fall into as the thought structure is transcended is warm and fulfilling all by itself. But it is also a place of potential creativity capable of manifesting new forms of service and love.

Dale: I like that.

I do too.

Mary: Often sitting in these circles with you, the whole front of my body becomes warm or even hot in just the way Dale was describing. Is the heat an edge where the force or the energy meets the resistance?

The heat functions like a fever. It burns off density and brings more openness or porousness to the body. It is healing. After the fever has done its work, we may experience a consistent warmth in the frontal membrane, the heart and the area around the heart. That warmth is our emotional life when stripped of all demands from the past.

The intense heat burns off that which is dense and obstructed. It opens passageways. It relieves inflammation and congestion in the subtle and invisible arenas of the bodily form and its radiant field.

As the body becomes tempered, the heat moderates and becomes a steady warmth. But even the word "warmth" is a little confusing here because it is more like a breeze — very soothing and gentle. That warmth is compassion, a deep attraction to life — Eros.

3

So there you are with yourself
in a tight, lonely space
beating up the one
who is in pain.

Linda: I would like to talk about feeling hurt. I've heard you say before, "What is wrong with being hurt?" I just don't get that. To me it's a crazy question.

I live with someone who is very different from me and we start hurting each other very easily. I withdraw and then I think I'll speak to her later about the hurt and then I decide it's not worth bringing it all up again or getting more hurt. Then I come back to the question of why do I fear getting hurt so much?

But that's a very important question. It's not a question that's very often asked because the assumption is that hurt is simply something we don't want. So I pose the question to you because you are bringing up your direct experience: Why do you feel tense about being hurt? What is it that makes you tense in the experience?

Linda: I think maybe it's that I'm afraid I'll get out of control and scream and get angry and pile more hurt on.

Is that what you think or is that what you know?

Linda: I don't know anything.

That's a guess then?

Linda: Yes, that's a guess.

So, we sit like this for a while and then we ask: When you feel this hurt, where do you feel it?

Linda: I feel it in my heart. I feel as if I've ruined a peace. I want everything to be right and I want everything to be peaceful and I want everybody to be happy.

Do you recognize the difference between feeling hurt and having those thoughts? Do you see that they are not the same thing — that feeling hurt and having that series of thoughts are two different internal events? The thoughts are an attempt to explain, but the hurt itself is something different.

Let's go back to the body. What is it about being hurt that you don't like?

Linda: It's very hard to describe. I would say, who wants pain?

I'm just exploring with you. I'm not trying to make a point. Are you sure it's pain?

Linda: It feels like pain.

It feels physically like pain. Do you try to get away from it or the circumstances that seem to be causing it? Are you suggesting that when I ask what is wrong with being hurt that I am suggesting we should stay in situations that are hurting us? Is that part of the confusion?

Linda: I feel like I'm missing something. When you ask me that question, I feel there's something I don't understand. To me, that pain is wrong and being hurt is wrong. It's not the way that I want or expect to be.

But you are sometimes.

Linda: Yes.

You use the word "wrong" deliberately. Is it wrong to be hurt?

Linda: I don't know, maybe unnatural. My natural state is to be happy.

But is that the state you find yourself in?

Linda: No, I've gotten away from that.

Then, on what basis do you conclude it's natural to be happy?

Linda: I don't know.

I mean it's a thought. I'm not saying it's not a correct thought. I'm simply asking you what evidence you have to conclude unhappiness is unnatural?

Linda: Here I am. It feels right.

It feels right that you should be happy and it feels wrong that you're not. So, when you're not happy that means that you're wrong?

Linda: Yes. I think also that it feels that I could have corrected it. If I'd chosen to use different words, I could have avoided the whole thing.

You could have avoided your hurt if you had done something different. So, what we come down to, as we begin to work through this, is that getting hurt is one experience. Then a secondary experience emerges which encircles the hurt — that is, an attack or self-blame. If you were more successful at human relations there would be no hurt.

Linda: Yes.

Which is more painful — the hurt of the relationship or the self-attack?

Linda: The attack.

So there you are with yourself in a tight, lonely space beating up the one who is in pain. You ask me the question about what is wrong with being hurt, but you clearly think that not only is being hurt wrong, but it is a personal failure.

We have a child who comes home at the end of the day and is hurt by something that happened at school and we take him into the room and beat him up. You would be the first person to reject that as a solution. It would be unthinkable to you. It would be an outrage beyond reckoning because your code of justice is so strong. But what about this?

Linda: I've never even thought about it that way.

It's so unconscious that you don't see how you're treating yourself. This is the way you try to get rid of feeling vulnerable — by beating yourself up. Now, it may be natural to be happy, but is it natural to hit yourself when you're not?

Linda: No, I would consider that to be very cruel.

Very cruel. We're hurting because of a certain delicacy, because we feel vulnerable, alone, like somehow someone doesn't love us or we're not loved. This is very rough.

We hurt because we don't feel loved and we want to. We hurt because there is a loneliness and a longing in the heart. Then we beat ourselves up. Where did that particular solution come from?

Linda: I don't know.

I don't either. It doesn't even matter. The actual insight mechanism is useless in the face of such an approach to ourselves. In our process, we just look at the choreography of this cruel dance. Why is there a problem with being delicate?

Let's say that it is easy for you to get hurt, that you are vulnerable to the sting of strong words, or whatever. Does that mean that there is something wrong with you? Is that a weakness?

Linda: I wouldn't consider it a weakness in anyone else.

But in you, it's not only a weakness, it's an offense that's punishable. Isn't that true?

Linda: Yes.

Some of us are wounded in a way that makes it harder to put up a defense and, in your moral code, that undefended aspect is wrong.

Linda: This person I'm talking about is my adult daughter. On top of all of that, I also can see that what I do is I give myself a message that if I had been a better mother, then she wouldn't be getting so upset and we wouldn't be into this.

Now, is that true or is that an opinion? And if you think it is true, how did you come to that idea?

Linda: Well, because of all the mistakes I made as a mother.

Let's just look at that a little bit. How do you know they are mistakes?

Linda: Because I felt so often I wasn't doing what I should. I was out of control. I wasn't coming from the place of love. I couldn't come from the place of love all the time. I felt so bad when I couldn't do that. I felt so bad.

Of course.

Linda: They were children and they needed to be cared for.

That's right. I know what you are saying and I certainly don't make light of it. I understand that sometimes we can look back on our past and see things we did that we are not absolutely fulfilled about.
    But now this child still comes to you and gets the same lack of care, the same abandonment that you were just describing to me.

Linda: What did you say?

A child still comes home, inside your heart, and gets the same treatment. When does it stop? Until you've paid the price for what you did? When does it end? Is it any better to continue to do it to yourself than it was to do it then?

A person carries some sense of regret about their relationship to the children. We were hard on them, perhaps, when it would have been kinder to be soft. Sometimes we were harsh and even out of control. Things do happen and there are times, particularly after we've grown a lot, that we look back and understand that we were contracted, afraid and uneasy with ourselves. We were in pain. We were unable to do what seemed to be the highest at the time.

But then we keep doing it to ourselves. So the question becomes — are you worth less than they are? Or is this in some way a compensation for the past? Is this a mechanism which whips out of control or do you think it is something that could be stopped?

Linda: I feel out of control because I can see that I'm not as hurt as I used to be, but I'm still surprised that I stopped being hurt in the work place. The minute I step across my own door that hurt is there. I'm still so vulnerable.

Vulnerability makes you terribly afraid. In the face of what's vulnerable you think you're going to lose control. When you consider the relationship between mother and child, for instance, clear lines of delineation fade. Their pain is yours at a certain level. When they are vulnerable, it becomes yours and frightens you deeply.

There is even a tone of violence in your response to vulnerability, particularly when it's close to home. Maybe not so much when it's not close to home. In the social, political scene you take on an ideology which is the opposite. Your ideological position, politically, is completely opposed to the way you treat yourself. People shouldn't be treated cruelly. The ideological position is a compensation, an ideal that you propose to everyone else except you.

Linda: What did you say about the violence?

What I hear is that when you're hurt and there is that vulnerability, that pain and that loneliness, then your reaction is almost violent. You start to hit and get out of control.

Linda: Yes, that's true.

You seemed to indicate that this violence affected your relationship with the children when they were young and that even now you use the fact of the past to brutalize the present. Do you think you can stop?

Linda: Over the years, there's been a healing. I have dialogues with myself and try to get myself back on track. Now when I beat myself up, it doesn't last as long.
I can see when I'm doing it now. I'd really like to stop.

Let's say you stop beating yourself up — what do you do with the hurt? Let's say you have another argument with your daughter and you feel hurt. What do you do now if you actually give up that particular self-attack? What do you do with the hurt?
  Let's say that it's natural to be happy, but let's say you're not happy because you hurt. What is a sign of self-respect in relationship to hurt?

Linda: To honor it or respect it, I guess.

Is there another alternative? To fight it and reject it?

Linda: I don't know. Is there?

Do you know what it might mean to honor and respect your hurt?

Linda: It's very hard for me to know that.

That's clear in that your response to it is violent. It's hard to honor something that we would like to beat up. At this moment you don't know how to honor your hurt. Hurt is connected to a moral tone, a judgment and an idea of right or wrong. Somebody was wrong and somebody was right and usually it was you who was wrong.

Let's say that you were wrong. Let's say that you could have done it better. Is that a justification for beating yourself up?

Linda: No.

Even if you were wrong, even if all the evidence pointed to the fact that you could have done it better, you would still have to learn how to honor and respect your hurt. The argument that it was your fault or that you could have done it better is not a justification for self-abuse.

Let's say that there's no talking to yourself, there's no talking yourself out of it. There is a hurt that you feel in the body and you weep if you need to and you touch the location of the hurt with your hand. You wait and stay easy. You allow it to be. Do you think that would be a mistake?

Linda: No, it sounds very simple.

Very simple. I'm allowed to hurt. I'm also allowed to be wrong. I'm allowed to have made mistakes. I'm allowed to have regrets. I'm allowed to care for myself.

Linda: I remember one time you asked me if I cared for myself and I really didn't know what to say.

It's a very big question. There's so much dilemma-making around hurt, so much confusion. The mind begins to invent battle lines, creates an urgency to take sides. This is not compassion.

Linda: It's very hard for me not to sit in judgment.

Particularly about something so soft as hurt feelings.

Linda: Most of the time both my daughter and I get hurt, not just one of us.

I'm sure that's true. You're both hurt. It's understandable. The chances are that the arguments you two are having are about the past in some disguised form.

The chances are that the guilt you feel in relationship to what is being covertly discussed would suggest a need for punishment. Sometimes we have a discussion between an adult and a child which is about making up for something which seemed to happen in the past, even though that discussion seems to be about a current situation. It is an attempt, often on the child's part, to find compensation. The discussion is so veiled that guilt and remorse tend to dominate but in the background.

I would be willing to wager that the arguments, if the guilt weren't as strong, would not be as painful or as long as they are now. Your need to engage is a reaction to the feelings which have been exposed as a result of her complaint, even though they seem to be about something else.

Do we achieve happiness by avoiding hurt?

Linda: It's a side track.

It sure is. Not only do you feel hurt but there is also a great sense of guilt. Those two things sit side by side. What do you feel now in your chest, in your heart? What do you feel now?

Linda: I feel the beginning of a peace.

A sense of relief.

Linda: I think I want to understand why I fear the hurt so much.

I could perhaps give you an anecdotal or philosophical statement in relationship to your question, but you would still feel hurt.

Linda: Yes, I want to know how not to feel hurt and you're saying just be with it and I'll find out that it's not as bad as I think.

Very much so, and that the hurt itself is asking for tenderness and you're not responding in that way. Therefore, it won't heal. It won't go away.

The hurt is saying that it wants your tenderness and you are saying, "Get out of here, go away. I don't like you. It is wrong to feel this way."

Linda: I get it.

The attitude you take toward hurt is probably a part of a survival mechanism that seemed necessary in the past, but it bears no relationship to the present. It is no longer useful.

Linda: The secret is out.

The secret is out. "I want to be taken care of sometimes."

Linda: I had to keep that in for so long.

Of course you did and the way you dealt with it was not wrong. It's simply no longer appropriate.

Linda: Thank you, Steve.

4

**There is nothing
you can tell yourself about pain
that will heal it.**

Melissa: I experience a lot of fear about time. Anything with a deadline can bring on a panic. If I have to get papers ready for school or catch an airplane, I get thrown into a terrible anxiety. I wish I could come to a better agreement with time. I never seem to have enough time.

Planning and organizing this workshop gave me a great deal of anxiety. But now as I sit here, I feel good about everyone and what's going on.

You don't feel anxious right now.

Melissa: No.

I hear what you are saying and I respect it. However, one of the most difficult aspects of working with people in some healing role is that it is virtually impossible to deal with an issue or difficulty that's over.

Maybe it's just the limitations of my own perspective, but I draw a blank when a question is brought up which relates to something that doesn't exist right here. We would have to go into a fantasy to work with an anxiety that you are not feeling right now.

I'm not saying that you asked a wrong question. I'm not being critical in any way. A meeting such as this one should be an encounter with what exists here, and not an attempt to deal with a fantasy.

Melissa: That makes perfect sense. It's been a pattern for my whole life, and I don't know what to do about it.

I totally respect that. It's true, though, that you can hear the difference in the tone of a person's voice when they are trying to deal with something that is, at that moment, an abstraction. It sounds less connected to the body, a little tighter.

When we have experienced something over and over again as a pattern and are not experiencing it at this moment, then our urge to solve it must be oriented toward a future time and place. Making an attempt to solve something that we know once occurred and that we assume will occur again, creates an unsettled relationship to the present.

We actually have to reconstruct the past and invent the future in order to begin dealing with the so-called issue of your anxiety about time. Such an invention can be very confusing because all the solutions must be conceptual, in the head, and not organically arrived at.

If we were to pursue your anxiety about time in the way you initially wanted to, it would eliminate the possibility of a living encounter, an experience outside the frame of reference which is causing the conflict in the first place. We would get kind of stuck.

When the orientation is toward solving something that we remember occurring in the past and then anticipating its reappearance in the future, we lose sight of the real motivation that has drawn us together. We want to have an encounter in the present which is outside the usual ways of defining ourselves. If we attempt, as our sole purpose, to deal with an experience that doesn't actually exist at this moment, we begin to travel down a road which can lead us into very perplexing misunderstandings.

We are here together. Some vital possibility exists which can't be fully understood from a conceptual frame. You have brought up a difficulty which arose a few days ago, but somehow your desire to communicate holds a more profound opportunity than simply discussing the problem as you remember it.

Let's begin to settle into our experience together as it is. Notice the body. Stay easy with it. Breathe and allow. If there is tension somewhere, uneasiness, discomfort, just breathe and give it permission.

We are looking for an actual experience. Ideas solve very little when it comes to the realm of our internal experience. We want to get outside the frame of reference which is causing the conflict and making us uptight.

When you speak about time, or any other condition, you are really speaking about a locater, a frame of reference, which is by its very nature limited. Each of us has access to an explosive, expansive space which we are keeping at bay. This space is non-conceptual; it is not governed by the ideas we use to cage ourselves in so much of the time.

Whenever people tie themselves down to any particular frame of reference, it is inevitable that conflict will arise. Whenever we clutch to an image, negative or positive, and thereby avoid the space that lies outside, beyond that image, we are going to collide with walls. We are also going to find that we long for that which is free of conceptual references, while we hide inside an appearance.

Deep within, we are looking for a way to come into something different, something outside of conflict and predicaments that have no solution on the level at which they appear. We begin by coming to the body as it is, in a relaxed and gentle way. We let the whole body be easy, consciously experiencing the breathing and staying attentively open to what is.

How does your body feel?

Melissa: I have a sense of everyone breathing together. I feel very much at one with you and everybody here. I feel quite comfortable, a little tingly and relaxed.

Can you allow your attention to be with me through the front of your body for a few minutes?

Melissa: Yes.

Do you feel us together? Do you feel me with you?

Melissa: I don't know. I can't really describe it. I'm staying with my body and breathing, not expecting anything. Yet I want something.

Is the wanting a feeling or is it an idea?

Melissa: It's an idea. I really feel very much at ease.

Do you have any problems?

Melissa: On the thinking level, I do.

Right this minute?

Melissa: Right now, I don't feel like I do. I could remember what the problems are, but they don't come easily.

In the experience at this moment, there is no problem?

Melissa: No.

And you haven't had an insight nor have your outward circumstances changed.

Melissa: That's right.

You are exactly the same person who you were before, except that you don't have any problems.

Melissa: I've been feeling that a lot today.

You and I both know, for better or for worse, that somewhere down the road, you are going to perceive yourself as a person who does have problems. But at this moment you are having an actual experience of living with yourself without dilemmas or difficulties.

Melissa: Yes, that's true. But I really do have lots of issues.

They are waiting for you somewhere.

Melissa: Yes.

Can you conceive, as you sit here, of the possibility of entering into your life without the dilemmas? Does it feel like a remote possibility that you could leave here and have none of the troubles that disturbed you before?

Melissa: That seems so far out. Would I be walking in a haze or some other odd state?

Do you feel clear right now or do you feel hazy?

Melissa: I feel clear.

Since your life hasn't changed and nothing in your environment has changed, where are the problems?

Melissa: They are in the future or the past.

They simply and truthfully don't exist at this moment.

Melissa: Right.

But when they do exist, can you locate experientially where they occur?

Melissa: Yes, they cause pain and worry and arguments about how to deal with them.

Do the circumstances which usually cause you pain have that pain inherent to them? Are they inherently problems or is the problem the fact of the pain?

Melissa: I'm not sure I understand.

Is there something inherently problematic about the circumstances which causes your pain? Or is the pain itself the cause of the dilemma and not the circumstances? If you didn't have the pain, would there be conflict about the circumstances?

Melissa: Probably not.

So when you say to me that there are circumstances which cause you pain, you are really saying that the fact of your pain causes confusion and conflict, not necessarily the circumstances?

Melissa: I think that's true.

If the circumstances weren't causing you pain, if you felt clear even with certain events going on, while there might be decisions to make, there wouldn't be the kind of suffering or struggle that you usually experience around them.

Melissa: I'm trying to understand.

I'm saying that part of your conflict is about pain and not circumstances. It's the pain itself that is so troubling.

Melissa: I have a grown child that needs money. I feel guilty, give her the money and then feel angry because I think I have been manipulated. I can't free myself of this cycle. I don't want the responsibility anymore. It's all old stuff.
  I have another grown child who sort of cut himself off from me and that hurts when I think about it.

It's the hurt that you don't like and not the fact that he cut himself off?

Melissa: That's right.

This is very important. When you look at the difficulties you are having in life, it is not the circumstances you don't like, it's the pain.

Melissa: Yes, and the conflict of feeling guilty.

The conflict is a little different from the pain. You are experiencing something in your body that you don't feel comfortable with, and the conflict relates to how you can maneuver the outside so that the feeling will go away. Isn't that true?

Melissa: Yes.

When you speak about a child who has cut himself off from you or demands money, there is nothing objectively conflicting about those events. It's that those circumstances evoke a pain that you don't like.

Melissa: I understand. I got you.

When you have conflict, struggle, when you don't know what to do, it's not about the child who demands money, etc., but rather about how to deal with your own pain.

Melissa: You are right. This is so great. I want to know how to deal with the pain.

The child who makes you feel manipulated is trying to solve her own pain through you, and so you are trying to solve your pain through her. This is not a criticism at all. It is an observation.

We are all, on one level or another, trying to deal with our own pain by trying to get someone else to behave differently.

Melissa: This is instead of coming to the pain warmly?

If I were able to magically take away the pain whenever your children behaved in a certain way toward you, the fear and the confusion about what to do would go away. You would know what to do. It's really not the circumstance that you are struggling with. It's what to do about your own reaction.

You are looking at the way in which reality is invented by the mind. There is no objective conflict in your relationship with the children. While you try to solve your own pain by dealing with them, you are creating a phantom reality which only appears to be objective.

Our whole concern in this life is Narcissus. We are looking out at others and seeing in them a reflection of our own concerns or pain. We are not really trying to help them; we are attempting to deal with ourselves.

Melissa: This is especially true with one's children.

They are capable of evoking a lot of guilt and confusion. At the same time, however, we can see that at least in part we don't want anything "bad" to happen to our children because we don't want to experience the pain. There are other elements, of course, but we must be able to observe this one if we are to be honest.

Melissa: I see that in myself.

If we knew that we were going to respond to our own pain with compassion, warmth and softness, there would be less glueyness in our intimate relationships.

Compassion for another person is quite different from the panic which occurs when we are using someone else to deal with our own pain. It is enormously empowering to understand that the pain is not being caused by an event which is objectively pain-causing. The pain has been evoked. Our obsession about how to deal with the event relates more to our own body than anything else. We don't like the pain.

But who doesn't like the pain? Where does this "not liking" come from? Can we observe the difference between the pain and not liking the pain? We might assume that not liking pain is inherent to the pain, but when we slow things down a bit, we can see that the pain is occurring in one location and the "not liking" is occurring in another.

The pain is not inherently conflicted. It can be clear and steady. A conflict did get imposed onto that pain. The idea makes the pain appear conflicted. "I don't like this pain," is a conflict. It is an assumption that what is happening in the body is wrong or foreign.

"I don't like the pain," is an irritant to the pain itself. When the "not liking" is fiercely fastened to the pain, we may experience both events as if they were the same.

When we shift toward that space in which the problem doesn't exist, even though there may be pain, we discover that the part of ourselves which does not like the pain is different from the pain itself.

"I don't like the pain," is the imposition of a conditioned response onto something which is occurring in the body. When we don't like the pain, our perception of it is immediately distorted. It becomes more difficult and demanding than it actually is.

The primary problem that you are having with your children is that they are evoking pain in you, and your mental reflex is to not like that pain. You respond to it as if it were a foreignness, a disease. The body creates a peculiar defense against an innocent experience. It tightens down and holds back.

Each of us has been taught to resolve this kind of pain by either manipulating the circumstances or by manipulating ourselves. We manipulate ourselves by tightening the body and using it as a mechanism of suppression and also by creating concepts, story lines and ideas which are fantasized substitutes for self-care.

We think that we are struggling with our husband, wife, child, etc., but we are actually struggling with our own body. The reason that we don't know how to appropriately serve that person is because we don't see them. We see only our own pain. We are trying to get rid of something we don't like by dealing with someone else as if they were the cause.

From a particular paradigm, it seems natural and obvious to dislike pain. The "not liking" is rarely questioned or understood to be different from the pain itself. The pain is a subtle physical event which can't be fully dealt with through either insight, self-manipulation or pushing circumstances in certain directions.

The approach to the interplay between pain and circumstance that we take here is different from the one which is habitually taken most of the time. We don't know what to do about our child, etc., because we are not feeling warmth toward ourselves. If there were the kind of warmth toward self that we experience in this circle, what steps to take and how to serve appropriately would be relatively clear.

The healing that you seek has little to do with your children and the mental conflict which seems to surround them. It relates almost entirely to how you are treating your own pain and the discovery that disliking it and trying to make it go away is the cause of your suffering at this point in time.

Melissa: Wow! I feel that.

We have not been given an education about how to deal with that bodily force that we call pain. We have been taught to treat it as a virus which must be eliminated synthetically, through some form of suppression or denial. We have not been taught why or how to take care of it. We've been taught to hate and distract, but not how to embrace and respect it.

Waiting, not doing anything for a certain period of time about the so-called external circumstance, is far more practical, more resilient with possibilities, than the struggle which has been going on for so long. The first step in self-care is to accept the way it is for even just a little while.

The initial impulse, when we are faced with pain, is to manipulate circumstances and ourselves. The initial impulse of emotional self-care is to leave the circumstance and attend to ourselves. There are some who might argue that such an approach is impractical and self-centered, even though years may have been spent obsessing in the same old way.

What you call reality is nothing more than a particular frame of reference; what your children call reality is their particular frame of reference. The actuality, although beyond words, can at least be described as much bigger than any particular frame of reference.

The frame that is used to define reality becomes a cage. It is a confinement. It isn't the objective circumstances that are causing the problem, but the fact of the frame itself. If we aim, in our problem-solving methodology, to deal with the circumstances that seem to be occurring within the frame, we can make only limited headway.

The process of opening ourselves into a deeper dimension, a different relationship to life, involves shifting the frame. The problem then begins to solve itself organically. The blinders are lifted. We can suddenly see more of what's really there.

If we drove our car with the windshield covered with ice and had only a small opening through which to view the road, driving would be experienced as a problem. If we never were shown anything else, we might assume that the car and all the mechanisms in it are inherently problematic. We might end up hating it, thinking that it's our unfortunate lot in life, our condition, our fate. If a hole were chopped in the ice and our view could be expanded, driving would have a different feel to it altogether.

It is so important to understand that the most sublime response to situations that are difficult for us is to wait and enter into ourselves warmly, openly, and then return when the perspective has changed.

Melissa: I am so moved because I was taught so thoroughly to hate my pain, to be tough and to keep a stiff upper lip.

In order to live that way you must tighten the body and live in thoughts of fear and doubt.

Melissa: The fear is so prevalent for me. I always think I must stay in control.

All you can actually control is your body and in the end that's what you are trying to control. It may appear as if you are trying to control the circumstances on the outside, but you are trying to control your own pain.

Melissa: I've always thought that pain is a sign of weakness and that I shouldn't be weak.

In that picture of yourself is a sense of shame about the body. The body is wrong and dangerous. It doesn't have a wisdom or a beauty. It isn't related to truth. The body is kept in chains.

Eros is dangerous. Life then becomes a technical struggle in thought. We miss the unfolding process, the holism of this life.

There is nothing that you can tell yourself about pain while it is occurring that is actually true. There is nothing that you can tell yourself about pain that will heal it. Pain is not healed by ideas. It can never be healed by adjusting our thoughts. Pain can't be solved by conceptual struggles with what is going on. Pain is healed by coming to it directly and attending to it as it is and not as we want it to be.

The pain does not leave; it is transformed. The very energy that lies at the base of pain is the energy that we want. It is the energy which gives us the strength to live. It is appearing as pain because of interpretation and contraction.

Melissa: Is the attacker, the one who hates the pain, an enemy?

To look at that voice as an enemy is to give it a reality and a strength which it doesn't inherently have. We simply offer the attention, the mother love, to our whole experience one step at a time.

As the attention is brought to the body in this way, that attacking voice stands little chance of staying alive as the demon, the dominant force. As long as it is given the energy of the fight, however, it seems to function as an independent force. It stabs at us, attacks and remains out of control.

Melissa: I know all this, Stephen, and I can help other people. But with myself it is so hard.

But as you learn to work with it in yourself, the ability to help others, in this regard, will dramatically increase. The depth and certainty of your relationship to this will be apparent to anyone who sits with you.

If you haven't resolved this in yourself, then a certain fear is going to pervade your approach to others, and the ability to relate in unflinchingly direct and unsentimental ways will not be as clear as it might be.

Melissa: You have helped me so much by just separating the hater from the pain and by giving me such an understanding of the frame. Thank you.

5

Our hurt becomes a door
into a different kind of reality.

Even though it may seem paradoxical, the truth is that if we are anxious, tense about something, fantasizing into the future, if we are obsessing, it is still possible to be easy with that experience, to just notice it and breathe.

One of the fundamental understandings of this work, of the process itself, is that a clean, non-evaluative observation is far more transformative than an insight. To observe the relationship between body and thought, not to do anything about it except offer it the conscious space of attention, allows an organic movement to take place which couldn't if we were looking for the insight or for some way to change.

Part of the reason why we close our eyes during the dialogues and the talks is to create an environment which is conducive to compassionate self-observation. It is, however, easy to lose the distinction between an observation and a comment. They aren't the same at all. An observation is a direct participatory entry of the attention into a particular event. A comment or an insight involves a conceptual frame which cuts off the movement and arrests organic growth.

It is vital, as we sit with ourselves, to let the attention be with the body, because it is far easier to notice the body in a non-evaluative way than it is to notice the mind's formulations. We just stay with the body and attend to the breath.

As we enter into the process, it is crucial to experience the breathing sensuously and not mechanically. Even if the breathing is tight, we attend to it. If we are in pain, or are having some other so-called emotional difficulty, we simply locate that experience physically and breathe.

The world of thought, of commentary and descriptions is a limited fragment of what is available to us. Coming to the body opens another possibility, a deeper sense of things. We begin to discover what is outside the fragment that we are currently identifying with. Such a discovery can not be made through manipulation or the pressure to change. It can only happen when we are open to what is.

We come to the body. We breathe. And in doing so we may notice some vulnerability, some tightness, some pain or even a sense of spaciousness, love. We stay with whatever we encounter. There is a definite distinction between what is occurring in the body and what we are saying about it from up above.

The body is not conflicted. It doesn't comment or describe. The body has no issues because it doesn't carry the past in the way the mind does. There is something occurring in the body, almost like a longing or a core that is seeking to expand and explode. Our relationship with this expanding, exploding force is often ambiguous. We have mixed interpretations about what it is and what it is for. Sometimes we try to push it away or press it into oblivion.

If we stay very quiet, however, and allow ourselves to explore on the subtlest level, we can find that all personal difficulties bear some relationship to this exploding force. Something within us is always trying to get beyond the confines we have created for ourselves. We don't want to be trapped.

Unfortunately, the sense that we don't want to be trapped is often dealt with by trying to get peaceful. But the radical notion we present as part of this process is that seeking peace in the face of discomfort is not the deeper purpose of the human journey. A spirituality which represents itself as a way to peace, where everything is calm, misses a beautiful and abundant possibility — that of coming into contact with what is making us restless and dissatisfied, coming to our energy.

Getting in touch with our restlessness, with the way life seems so limited, so bound and isolated — to ride it, feel it, move with it and not know what it means — is a great service to ourselves. It is an act of self-respect. But it is challenging because we have built up a fantasized scenario about what causes the restlessness and why it's there at all.

Each of us is a matrix of moving energies, both subtle and gross. These energies are naturally seeking to expand. They are constantly in process, never still. Sometimes they are experienced as a drive, a wanting, a problem, and sometimes they seem vaguer than that. There are times when we seem numb to them, make them flat.

There is great value in coming directly to our energies and in not merely seeking to find comfort or peace. Real movement develops when we can discover the body's energetic force aesthetically. We offer our attention to what is actually occurring and we wait.

As human beings we are in ferment, in process all the time. We often describe this ferment in perplexing and conflicted ways. Those descriptions are not necessarily the truth about what that ferment really is.

The spirituality that we move towards in this work is an activity of the attention in which the ferment of life, the movement, the perpetual urge to expand, is fully respected. But what is not respected, in this sense, is the way we have condemned and trivialized that urge, the way we have tried to put it away and make it wrong.

So much of the time we perceive ourselves as being caught inside the bodily frame, alone. We may notice that we perceive ourselves as encapsulated. As long as our perception of who we are is related to that encapsulation, there are going to be painful symptoms. And as long as thought is allowed to be the dominating influence on our perception, the symptoms of that perceived encapsulation are going to be interpreted in self-defeating ways.

We have a yearning to be free, to get out of the tight spot we seem to be caught in. This yearning is marvelous. It speaks highly of us as spiritual beings. We are yearning for freedom and love. An experience of the innocence of this yearning, its creative force, can arise only as a result of becoming conscious of the restlessness, the dissatisfaction, in a way that is free of repeated patterns of belief and thought.

Kathy: I would like to sit with you and explore, if possible.

That's great. Let's sit directly across from each other. Relax the body, close the eyes and be easy. I want to gently move through the rudiments of this process as we talk. I'm going to ask for your affirmation that what we are doing together is understandable and that you can actually do it.

When I say to you, for instance, bring your attention to the front of the body, is that natural and easy to do?

Kathy: It feels natural and easy.

And when you bring your attention to the front of the body, is there an experience there? Is something going on?

Kathy: My heart is pounding.

Can you notice that? Can you be aware in a simple way of your heart pounding?

Kathy: Yes.

Let's notice the aesthetic experience of your heart pounding, not making anything of it at all. Is your breathing stopped as you sit?

Kathy: No.

As you allow your attention to move beyond the pounding of your heart, are there other experiences in the front of your body?

Kathy: The whole area from my neck down to the front of my chest is clenched, almost like a cord right into my abdomen.

You experience that as a physical tightness, yes?

Kathy: Yes.

It is very important in speaking with someone during a subtle communication like this to recognize that, without a reeducation, most of us assume that tension is a feeling. Of course, it's felt. But in the process that we are unfolding here, a distinction is drawn between tension and feeling. You can say I feel the tension, meaning I am conscious of it. But a feeling is something else.
    It is also important to recognize that we are being given a beautiful opportunity when a person is able to identify fairly

clearly what the tension feels like, what its depth and direction are. Expressing the experience of tension in an artistic way offers a different view of it than our expression of it as a kind of cliche.

There is nothing wrong with having tension. It should not be treated like a problem. We want to fully participate in it instead of trying to force it away. We let the attention be with the tension.

Is that fairly easy, Kathy?

Kathy: I can feel it. I'm not comfortable with it, though.

In a sense you don't want to go near it like this.

Kathy: True.

Let me ask you this: When you don't want to experience tension, how do you try to avoid it? What is the internal method for stopping tension?

Kathy: Through a kind of restlessness, diversion of attention or sleepiness.

You either seek distraction or you seek sleep.

Kathy: Like unconsciousness.

In the experience you are having right now with the tension and the restlessness, are they different or are they the same?

Kathy: I think they are different but they fall on top of each other so quickly that I have a hard time delineating.

Which is on top of which in a physical sense? Is the tension on top of the restlessness or the other way around?

Kathy: The tension happens and the restlessness starts automatically.

Is the restlessness more pervasive than the tension? Does it take up more of your body?

Kathy: Yes.

The tension is localized and the restlessness is less so.

Kathy: Yes.

What is it about the restlessness that you don't like? What is it that makes the restlessness an experience you would rather not have?

Kathy: It's uncomfortable and it feels like there is never going to be a resolution. Even when I'm tired, it pushes me.

Now I'm going to make a more general comment. Please bear with me. We are speaking about the body and we are asking someone to describe aesthetically or artistically their bodily experience. It's important for the listener not to accept words that don't mean anything. There are words we all gravitate toward when expressing our experience. They aren't truthful even though they are commonly accepted as understandable truths.

Kathy said, "I feel uncomfortable." My next question would be, "What does uncomfortable mean?" Kathy began to answer that question when she said, "It feels like there is never going to be a resolution." An indistinct urge is permeating her body and it never finds resolution.

At this fundamental level, where a person is describing their body experience — their relationship to life current — we are well below the common metaphorical level.

The issues as they present themselves on the inside or the outside, in terms of content, are nothing more than metaphorical expressions of relationship to Eros, life current. While it may be useful and interesting to explore those metaphors, it is more fascinating and compelling to find the levels which are underneath.

Once we understand that Kathy is describing her relationship to life current and nothing else — the way in which her evolutionary process is unfolding and the way in which her full participation is being blocked — a real sense of dignity is restored. On the level of incidents, life events, we can easily feel humiliated by what seems to be going on.

At the energetic level, it doesn't have the same personal tone. It's part of a much greater process which encompasses far more than the simple dilemmas of one person's life.

Kathy is describing her particular relationship to life current as it tries to pour through her body. In understanding this, the spiritual or so-called psychological work simply offers the working tools for getting underneath the constraint of thought which is holding the life current back. The psychological symptoms are merely behavioral or metaphorical expressions of a subtle physiological event.

When you say, Kathy, that the restlessness never seems to resolve itself, you have given an important signal regarding your interpretation about the human experience. The question of when will it stop, when will everything finally be in place, is actually a demand which the mind makes on life. It is an impossible demand. Nothing will ever resolve itself. Nothing ever stops moving. Nothing will ever cease to be in a state of transition. That is the nature of life. The mind seeks resolutions, frames and organized pictures of what things will look like when this segment ends.

What you describe as the restlessness is a powerful movement within you, along with an attempt to stop it. Here is where we find ourselves as we speak. You feel restless. Energy is moving and it is being blocked, caged in. The habit pattern of mind is causing part of the block and is also trying to explain it. From this interplay arises an amorphous suffering, a hopelessness which I think you are familiar with.

Kathy: I am.

Let's go back to the body. Offer your attention to the body. Has there been any kind of shift or does it remain the same?

Kathy: As you spoke and I didn't have to be quite as present with you, it diminished somewhat. When you came back to me, it began again. I want up and out of this chair.

Is it only the chair? What would you do and where would you go?

Kathy: Nothing would resolve it. Nothing would make me feel better.

It's driving you?

Kathy: Yes.

Is there anything about the restlessness that you can say in an expressive or descriptive way that you haven't said as yet? Is there somewhere, for instance, where it's more intense?

Kathy: I feel it most in my chest and I want to physically push away.

How does the restlessness relate to what we might call anxiety? Is it surrounded by an anxiety or is it what you would call an anxiety in and of itself?

Kathy: (Silence) It's not similar to what I felt when I was having a lot of anxiety. The tension on my outer skin is the same. But the inner experience is different. I'm not having the same energy I did when there were a lot of panics.

The outer wrap is similar, but the inside is different.

Kathy: It's a heavy tightness.

But the restlessness is different from the tightness. It's underneath it?

Kathy: No. It feels like it's kind of beside it or even on top of it.

Can you offer your attention more substantially to the restlessness or do you have to offer your attention to the heaviness equally?

Kathy: I have to offer it to the tightness because I must breathe.

Without offering your attention to the tightness, it would be difficult to breathe.

Kathy: That's right.

Let's breathe together. In this experience, the mind makes comments. Is one of the comments something like, "It's hopeless. There is no way out?"

Kathy: Yes.

The thought that it's hopeless, with no way out, is a thread that runs through your life.

Kathy: Yes.

Is it possible, as you sit here, to recognize that the thought about hopelessness is an overlay? It isn't inherent to the restlessness or the tension.

Kathy: My experience has been in coming to this over the past year that there are periods of hopelessness and periods of extreme frustration. Sometimes I feel so near the end of it, at the edge of something.

When you feel yourself at the edge of something, does that come from the body? Do you know that in a deep way?

Kathy: Yes.

But when you are calling it hopeless, there's a shouting, angry quality to the voice. It's like saying, "I don't like you. Get away." The frustration, the sense of being at the edge of something and the hopelessness, the defeat, are coming from two different directions. One is a clamp-down in an extreme form and the other is a sensing of an impending explosion.

Kathy: Right now I feel close to the sense that something can happen, but there is also a wall. Part of me says, "Don't ever think you can get through this wall. It won't ever stop."

Let's go to this. But let me paint the picture with a broader stroke. Kathy is describing her relationship to an energy which is coming to or through the body. That energy is being prevented from doing what it apparently needs to do.

There are times when vital energy gets caught in webs of interpretive thought and we perceive it to be a foe. There are certainly times when we allow it to be a friend. When it's a foe, it feels like it wants to do something to us, to take over in a way that we can't trust. This same quality has a tremendous fascination for us on the other side. A part of us would really like to have it take over, to give up to it.

On the one side, our struggle seems to be with a force that wants to own us, to take over. It wants our submission. On the other side, we would like to do nothing more than give ourselves up to it. So much depends on the meaning we apply to what is going on. This is a spiritual experience. You are grappling with the question of autonomy and surrender, Eros and structure. You are struggling on an energetic level with creativity and form. When this is really known, experienced and understood in an organic way, it gives dignity and purpose to something which, right now, you would rather have go away.

We are sitting together facing into something that seems to want you. We are looking at the way you are trying to pressure that something into the mold of your beliefs and assumptions about life, to keep it under control. We are also exploring a force which seems outside of your control and a counter-force which also seems to be beyond your grasp.

When we look at our so-called internal life, it often appears to be taking place on its own. Sometimes it looks like a movement of forces over which we have no jurisdiction. There is a holdback and a moving force. You are watching. You are helpless in the face of it.

Rarely, if ever, can we deal with the issues and difficulties of life with the kind of free choice that we think is ours. Forces are operating through us which are not under our conscious and willful control. They threaten the notion that we are somebody in a separate, private way, that we have a cohesive and identifiable personal life. Just look at your thoughts. They come and go on their own. They are nearly impossible to subdue. The same is true of the life force, Eros. It works on its own. The illusion always is that this life is ours. It isn't. It is part of a great evolutionary process that we can resist or participate in, but never own or control.

Most self-help techniques arise from a picture of the human being which gives credence to the reality of free choice regarding the energetic movement within and around us. They are not based on an understanding which suggests that this life is only personal on one tiny edge. The rest of it consists of great evolutionary forces which we can only observe and attend to in certain ways.

We don't have the choice we think we have. We can't suddenly get over the ferment or the movement. There is not stillness on the level of form. There is a great stillness, but we can't come to it by trying to fight with movement.

Stay with the body. Just be with it in an easy way. Has there been a slight shift, Kathy?

Kathy: Yes.

You feel a little different?

Kathy: Yes.

We can literally follow the shifts another person is going through by being deeply attentive to our own body. I just felt a kind of attraction to Kathy. I could feel it as a more open, shared space. I could feel the relationship. Something new entered the domain of our exchange.

Whereas at the beginning, I could feel a hole or a gap between us and we were trying to reach across that hole, offering descriptions to each other. Now that hole feels less vacant, less empty. I feel you in a different way. Do you know what I mean?

Kathy: Yes, I do.

Let's stay with the body and with each other. Do you feel more space than you did a little while ago?

Kathy: It's almost like shelves fall through in the center of me and there is a kind of open space where I don't feel the same tightness.

Obviously, this doesn't mean that your struggle has gone away or that it's not there in the background. It's just that a certain spaciousness has arisen which wasn't there before. It is less definable.

When we are talking about health or neurosis, we are talking about relationship to space. By space, I don't mean vacancy. I mean presence or depth. When we are living in a way that might be described as healthy or balanced, we are living in a sense of space which is more expanded than the space that is squeezed by issues of thought and belief.

We stay with it. It's a bodily experience. It's just there. Do you feel any easiness in your heart?

Kathy: Some.

The rest of it is tight?

Kathy: Yes.

Do you think that it would be possible for us to go to the tightness together, to allow our attention to be with it as one?

Kathy: I have a desire to do it, but I'm a little afraid.

When you say that you are afraid to do it, does that mean there is a specific outcome that you fear? Are you frightened about something that you think will happen?

Kathy: I don't think about an outcome. It's very vague. A little part of me is cautious of how close I will let you get.

Do you feel pressured or cornered by me?

Kathy: A little off guard, but not cornered or pressured.

You mean that you don't quite know how to defend yourself against my presence?

Kathy: Yes.

Isn't there a combination of deep attraction to this encounter and also a fear, even a repulsion? You want and don't want it at the same time.

Kathy: Definitely.

Our relationship with intimacy is exactly the same as our relationship with life current. There is no distinction. The way we fight with Eros as it pours into this bodily frame is exactly the same way we are going to struggle with someone else in an intimate encounter.

What you and I are experiencing here is another effect of your own internal relationship to energy, but it is being expressed through our relationship. You are guarding yourself against this deeper meeting in the same way you guard against a full participation in the movement of life. At the same time you are enormously pulled to it. You are cautious, but not rigidly stopped.

Can you feel the desire to be loved?

Kathy: Yes, I never get it. I never let it in.

Somewhere down underneath there is an underlying statement or frame which suggests that an encounter such as this has a certain danger to it. And you react as if that danger is real and right at hand.

Because of our prior relationship and the trust we have developed, it is difficult for the mind to conceive of me as being really dangerous.

Kathy: That's true.

It's hard to find a story line which indicates that I am dangerous. But you partly respond to this dialogue as if I want something from you that you don't want to give. Even though there is no evidence, you respond as if there might be a real danger here.

Kathy: I get so close to it and then it leaves.

Stay with the body. Do you notice some place where you are tight, but not tight in the sense of tension, but rather where you feel separate or removed from the body's core?

Kathy: Yes, around the solar plexus. It's like I'm desperately trying to get away. There's a rod of tension which is off to the side a bit and creates a misalignment.

Here is such a beautiful opportunity. Just feel the misalignment in the body. Stay with it. You are familiar with this experience of being moved off to one side. Isn't this a reaction to relationship? You are trying to shift your body away so that you do not get exposed — almost as if by distorting your body in a certain way you'll avoid contact.

Kathy: My body wants to stop you.

And you can see that this is all taking place without any noticeable physical movement. You know that the intimacy is not about how close I am to you in gross physical terms, but it's about the way in which something is longing in each of us to melt together in a subtle, invisible way. The body is involved, but the intimacy is actually taking place in the living space between us. It has no distinguishable point of location. It's between us, in us and around us. But it is felt in the front of the body. In order to avoid intimacy, you must distort the frontal membrane.

You are trying to rubber-band your way out and you can feel that. It's a kind of squirming because you think that you are pinned. We are engaged in an important discipline because we are, by staying conscious of it all, not acting out the impulse to get up and run away.

Isn't it true that your response to our interaction is outside of conscious and willful control? You don't want to suffer in this way. It's just happening.

Kathy: That's the worst part. I don't seem to have any choice.

In the same way the intimacy is just happening. Have you disappeared in a way?

Kathy: I have to be very conscious of staying with you.

Where do you go?

Kathy: It's almost like I stand behind my body. I start shoving my body in front.

That something which you identify as "I" uses the body as a defensive wall.

Kathy: Yes.

So when you disappear, you're not really in your body in that sense. You are not using the body as an instrument of relationship, but rather as a defense.

Kathy: It feels like a tremendous disrespect for my body. I'm pushing my body.

You are responding as if intimacy were an assault. You need to protect yourself from it.

Kathy: I really see that.

The body is locked into a habit. This habit operates outside of our conscious control. That unique spaciousness which I call individuality, that which surrounds and fills the body, can actually dislocate from the body. The body is pushed forward like a wall and this presence, this hollow space, is held at bay. Using the body seems to protect you against the aggressive appearance of intimacy.

Can you observe this without making it wrong or bad?

Kathy: I can certainly see it, but because it's so uncomfortable I find it hard not to judge it.

You're in it right now.

Kathy: I can't get back into my body because the front part feels so tight right now. I can only get about half-way in.

Can you just look at this for a little while?

Kathy: I think so.

Here is the possibility of an observation which can be helpful. You find yourself in a particular relationship to the body. It hurts. You want something else on a conscious level. But that something else is not available through conscious and deliberate choice. We can't get away from how it is at this moment. Your only choice is to struggle or just to be here with it as it is.

Kathy: I can do it but I'm not sure what I'm being with. I can only feel the pain and the tightness in my chest.

Just be with that. In the background, isn't there a desire to beat it, punch it or get through it in some way? There's a rage.

Kathy: Right now I feel so delicate that I don't want to go near that rage.

The delicacy comes from the sense that the whole wall is being threatened?

Kathy: Yes.

Let's just sit together in silence for a while. I am allowing my attention to be with you through the front of my body. I don't lose myself in this, but I am completely with you.

Kathy: I feel a little looser in the front.

Is there less pain?

Kathy: No, just less struggle.

You feel more available again. You seem more here.

Kathy: I know, but I'm afraid that I'm going to leave again.

Your reaction to me was as if I were an aggressor. It seemed as if you were protecting yourself against an attack. You dislocated.

Kathy: So much of the time that dislocated place seems safe.

I understand that. But isn't there something else which seems to be forcing you away from that safety?

Kathy: Most of the time I think that I must stay like this because my environment, my life, is dangerous in a certain way.

Are you able to articulate the nature of the danger?

Kathy: I just need to defend my space. I think it's going to be taken from me.

Stay with the body. I'm going to allow my attention to be with you as you allow your attention to be with the front of your body.
   Your struggle on this level is about spaciousness. Is it safe to allow your own presence to be available in a general way? You tend to squeeze it back.

Kathy: I feel weighted. I don't feel sleepy, but it's like I'm sinking a little bit.

Let's go with the sinking. Let it happen. We are interweaving a communication about subtle energetic experiences while offering complete permission to have an experience without the veil of conceptual, personalized meaning.
   Participating like this reveals, in a direct and unsentimental way, a pattern of relationship that has been with you for a long time. Here is the entire movement, step by step, of your relationship to relationship.
   What we are looking at today goes on in the background during the normal course of your life. Surface content dominates and a clear picture of this phenomenon is lost. The struggle appears to be occurring as a result of what somebody else does to you or against you. It doesn't look like it's happening at subtle levels in your body. The actual location switches from your own body to a relationship with someone else. It gets vague.
   Our process here is a temporary entry into an unusual relationship with external reality. We are giving ourselves the chance to witness our internal life at a level deeper than the symbolic content we usually create to distract ourselves.

Unlike most of our common experiences, patience is paramount. Usually, patience is sacrificed to the symbol, to what is happening on the outside.

Our work here requires patience for all involved — to be with you as you come and go, to listen to descriptions of subtle body movements, to expect nothing. We ordinarily don't give each other such permission.

The healer, listener, friend — whatever term we want to use — is responsible for maintaining a space, upholding a space that makes it possible for all organic changes to occur.

What is your experience now, Kathy?

Kathy: I'm bored.

Is that familiar?

Kathy: Yes.

Is that a bodily experience?

Kathy: Yes.

Now if we were in relationship on the outside, wouldn't you assume that you were bored with me.

Kathy: Yes.

You are bored with the level of encounter that you are willing to come to. Do you know what I'm saying? You are keeping yourself at a point which is just distant enough for it to lose fascination.

Kathy: When I'm in relationship and this boredom comes, I begin to feel restless. I search for distractions and soon enough I leave.

It's important to see that. When you combine boredom with the restless desire to get away, it is very easy to say, "This relationship is over. The things that used to fascinate me about you are gone."

Kathy: I don't want this anymore.

Can you see that your struggle with this, your hatred of it, are not aimed at releasing you from it? The struggle has the opposite effect.

One of the major understandings of this work is that when we are in a struggle with an aspect of ourselves, we are actually giving it the strength to remain. The hate keeps it alive.

The way out, if you will, is a melt. It involves a de-structuring. The only movement available to us as human beings is melting movement. Mechanical movement is an illusion, a kind of theatrics which doesn't relate to organic process. All resistance is structural and mechanical.

Self-hatred, disliking and not wanting something about ourselves, maintains structure. Compassionate observation is real self-care. It doesn't manipulate change; it simply provides the opening for it to happen.

Today you can see an internal mechanism which seems to function with a great deal of autonomy. It includes hiding, running, tensing, distracting, dislocating, getting bored, etc.

Kathy: I feel so removed suddenly.

You mean that your body feels vacant again?

Kathy: Yes.

Do you feel an urgency to get over it?

Kathy: I'm just breathing with it.

You can hear how being removed even affects your voice. It has less power, less resonance. I am experiencing a longing for you. At the mind's level, if we were in a different kind of relationship, I would feel hurt at this point. This is the point at which someone else's pattern gets set off, especially if it's related to abandonment. I wouldn't be sure whether you are judging me or not, whether you really cared.

Kathy: I know. I was just about to say that I would start thinking that you want something from me that I don't want to give. I would think you were clinging to me.

This is interesting because the reason someone might start clinging to you at this point is because they've tasted you, touched you and found you in a genuine way, and then you left. They want you back, but they don't know how to find you.

Kathy: When they do start clinging, it's an affirmation that I really did need to protect myself. My interpretation becomes that the other person wants everything they can get and will leave me empty.

In the ordinary stream of events, the other person might also get angry because they are protecting their own hurt and because anger itself offers some possibility of opening you up again. To hurt you may break down the wall. Emotional hurt can bring a person back to the body.

Kathy: I just want to curl up, clinch down.

Someone might say, "Kathy, I love you but I don't know what to do with you."

Kathy: I kind of wave at them from the side as they walk away. I have been through this.

And then you tease them.

Kathy: Yes, I tease them just so much that they come back.

In ordinary relationship your disappearances, the hiding, could easily be interpreted as betrayal. I've loved you and loved you and now you have gone away.

Kathy: The person I'm with now at least says, "I know you are there. Please come out." I'd like to kill him for that.

It's a pressure, an assault. But when he actually does go away from you, you start longing for him again.

Kathy: This hurts so much.

It's a conditioned mechanism responding to a variety of forces. Most of the content is fantasy. The mechanism doesn't bear any particular relationship to what is happening in the present. It was formed in some other space and time. But when that was, and what circumstances actually caused this reflex to begin coming into play, is irrelevant. Insights like that don't heal. Only the space of self-acceptance does.

Kathy: I feel that.

This is a mechanism of self-protection. You are responding to whoever is with you in the present as if the whole event were taking place somewhere else, in some other frame.

One of the earmarks of the kind of hiding that you engage in is a repulsion for the person you assume is pursuing you. Suddenly all their characteristics, even the ones that had once fascinated you, become ugly.

Kathy: Almost sickening at times.

Come back to the body. The whole mechanism that you are facing right now might be called a tendency. It isn't related to you in a personal way even though it has personal overtones. It is like an independent drive. The tendency constitutes the way in which we manufacture reality on this planet. It is the blinders we wear that give us a particular angle on what is going on here.

Something is going on in this world, but it's not the same as the reality frame in which you live. All of us make up the same relationships over and over again. And interestingly enough, we always seem to find a person who is willing to cooperate with us in an exquisitely matched way. It's so mysterious, almost uncanny.

We could say that until we have melted out of the tendency, transcended it through love, the other people in our lives don't exist as independent entities. They are just a part of our fantasy — and vice versa. We don't know who they are.

We were attracted at first by a moment with them in which the tendency had not yet come into play. They seemed so interesting and fresh. Soon after that, the myth takes over and it takes a lot of work to come back.

Where do you find yourself, Kathy?

Kathy: I feel a little bit tight, but more present.

Come to the body again and feel, allow. Do you feel something in your body, Kathy?

Kathy: I can feel my body differently. I feel bigger, more expanded.

Let's come to the heart together. Allow your attention to be open to me through the body. It's there again, isn't it?

Kathy: Yes, I feel like a woman.

There is something else now between us, an aliveness, a softness that we can both feel. It's not that there are no boundaries, but just that the boundaries are out farther than they were before.

Your boundaries remain but there is also another dimension of silence, of space, that we have passed into. It's now hard to distinguish between my feeling you, your feeling me and feeling ourselves. A melt has begun to happen. Do you feel that?

Kathy: Yes.

It's like there is one space now. And while I remain who I am in some background way, I am clearly not different from you. When I say that I love you, do you know what I mean? Something is beautifully alive which has nothing to do with the constrained limits of personality and belief. I love you because we are together, because we have found the common space.

Do you feel afraid?

Kathy: No, but there is a voice in the back of my mind suggesting I should be cautious. I do feel present though.

When you had the thoughts about caution, could you notice that there was a different spatial relationship to these thoughts from what there usually is? They didn't seem quite as oppressive as they ordinarily do.

Kathy: They sort of haunt me in the background.

One of the aspects of the squeezed position in life, when thought dominates and the body is used as an instrument of defense, is that thoughts seem to take up most of our available space. There isn't any room for a more expansive awareness of self. In this deeper modality, thoughts are there but they aren't taking all the available space. They don't trap us in the same way. This changes all our relationships.

Kathy: I feel that.

Once again, let's go to the body and open the attention through the body to each other. Can you feel that?

Kathy: Yes, even though it feels fragile.

I understand.

Kathy: My chest still hurts, but there is much more there. I feel much easier, a lot more present.

I wonder if there is anyone else who would like to enter into this dialogue with a question or an expression of feeling?

Arthur: You were describing how, if you were in some ego place, you would have felt hurt when you sensed Kathy's withdrawal, but it didn't hurt from the place you were in then. Was it easy to handle perhaps because you are not in a committed relationship with Kathy?

This all brings up a dilemma for me. I experience my wife's withdrawing in that way; and at that point in time, since we are in a committed relationship, I just don't know what to do. I withdraw, get angry, feel helpless and hopeless. None of this is to blame her. I realize I'm speaking about my own dilemma.

I can't quite get at the question.

I think I hear the question. When someone withdraws and we feel hurt, the question is not about the person who withdrew, but rather about our relationship to hurt. Otherwise, the question becomes how can I get my partner to come back to me or to behave in a way that doesn't make me hurt?

The question isn't about your wife. The question comes back to mother in a solid way. This is not a psychological theory which suggests that your wife has become a symbol of your mother. It is rather how to bring the mothering process to yourself, now that the wound has been exposed.

The hurt that you are experiencing, the wound, was not created by your wife's withdrawal. It was there. When she behaves in a certain way toward you, the wanting in the wound seems to go away. But when she withdraws her attention from you, the wanting in the wound comes raging back.

All this comes right down to the question of how you can offer to yourself that which your wife seemed to be offering before. What are the skills or approaches necessary to attend and care for yourself? This is one of the most intense challenges we can ever face. It's like riding a wild horse because something inside is insisting that the pain is about someone else. And that something has the glow of reality to it. We have been in partnership with that voice for so long that when it says, "Who are you kidding? This is about my wife and I have to get her to see it my way," you believe it. That belief manufactures a reality myth which is based on one particular viewpoint.

There is another side to this which is based on the understanding that you must get through the myth that this is about Elizabeth, and come to the feeling openly even though part of you aches to make it about her.

Arthur: The implication of what you are saying is that we really are alone.

You certainly are alone in the paradigm that is creating the problem. The paradigm of separateness forces us into peculiar dependencies on each other. It manufactures a reality frame which is oriented to complete isolation. The desire for intimacy seems unclean and unclear. We have to strategize and manipulate to get what we are longing for.

Arthur: What is the alternative?

We turn toward our pain and enter into our woundedness directly. We just stay with it and breathe. Through this we discover that the wound is a raw and injured passageway that we have been taught to demean and negate. As we keep opening to it, that wound becomes a place where we can find someone in a way that we have never done before. We begin to transcend the separateness through this deep and immediate self-care.

The only way that our wounds can be healed is by bringing mother love to ourselves, by bringing the nurturing force to our own being. This means attending to it. Attending to the hurt is different from loving it. We can't decide to love something. Love is not part of conscious choice. We attend to the wound and love unfolds from the place that once hurt — from the body and not from thought.

Attending to hurt involves breathing with it, staying with it, lifting off our ideas about it and releasing all the pressure to get rid of it, to change it, to get to the other side. The hurt becomes a door into a different reality, a different paradigm.

Arthur: I really hear what you are saying, but to do it is another matter.

You are having an infant response to mother. All our relationships to hurt are reflective of primal exchanges at various points in our development here, there and elsewhere. The response of needing someone to stroke us when we hurt is entirely appropriate at one point in time and then is less appropriate at another point in time.

Learning how to open into mother, into the nurturing essence which is around us and within us is the next step in the evolutionary process. It is spiritual. That hurt, that wound, is a prayer because instead of relying on the infant need for physical mother, we turn our longing toward the universe itself. We turn toward something greater than what we conceive ourselves to be. We do this through self-respect, by treating the wound as a sacred passageway.

Arthur: Can you expand on that a bit?

We begin by turning our attention to the hurt as a prayer. We allow the body to pray. Our hurts and wounds are entry points into a different and deeper dimension. In that dimension we encounter forces, intelligences which can communicate to us or through us on a feeling level.

The pain and the hurt are a doorway into a different kind of space, a different terrain. We rarely enter that terrain because we don't allow ourselves to discover the passageway that the hurt represents.

Arthur: Let me pursue this a little more. What are the forces that you are alluding to? I know, ultimately, they can only be experienced, but I need to know more.

Please take this at whatever level you want to or don't take it at all. I am not interested in creating a belief structure or a philosophical demand.

The perceptual paradigm which has been indoctrinated into us is one of tight aloneness inside the physical body. We experience this life as if we were caught inside a material frame, looking out, fearing death and change. From this paradigm, we can't know whether there is any interactive relationship between ourselves, for instance, and the stars in the sky. We assume that we must struggle this life out pretty much alone.

To the one caught inside the body there are comforts, discomforts, pleasures and pains. We perceive ourselves as dwelling in a very limited cage.

One of the things that we intuitively sense, even when we are in this tight relationship to life, is that there is more to it than what we currently know. And we long for that. We know inside that there is something more to this life experience than simply waiting it out for seventy years.

We also sense sometimes, when we are quiet and open, that we are not as separate from each other as it seems. Just beyond the edge, there is another possibility. It has been suggested for millenniums, in many spiritual traditions, that intelligent presences, conscious presences, guide and work with the evolution of humanity. One could call these intelligences forces, beings, guides or any other metaphor that makes sense.

It is clear even in a so-called rational framework that different levels of reality function differently and have different forces working through them. There are forces which work on or stimulate evolution. The responsibility, the task of being on this earth, is to work with these forces, these guiding energies, by disbanding the whole system of belief which blocks us from the connection.

Invisible intelligences can communicate to us in just the way we communicate with each other — through the frontal membrane. These communications are energetic exchanges which are received and given through the body's subtle membrane. What we tend to do, as a result of the way we are glued to the present paradigm, is fix personal and often trivial meanings onto these deep communications as if they were our emotions, our weaknesses, etc.

The goal is to cease applying personal, superficial meanings to our communications with energetic realms outside, and to begin discovering what is really there. We enter into the feeling because it is a wisdom-bearer. We listen to what it says.

This universe is not a linear, orderly system of appearances. It is rather a whole, a multi-dimensional curve of possibilities taking place on different levels. Within this curve, there are greater and lesser forms of intelligence. Different forms of intelligence are involved at different levels of evolution. Some of those intelligences, in their compassion, turn toward the human being, and assist in a non-intrusive way. Interestingly enough, the way to turn toward them is through the prayer of acceptance and self-respect.

Arthur: These then are not impersonal forces? Why do you use the word compassionate?

The kind of compassion, for instance, which is being offered to you by the universe is a very different, less personal compassion than I could offer to you. It keeps ribbing you, riding you and forcing you to face into something that you would rather not face into.

Life does not follow the moral structure that we would like it to. Its purpose is obviously not the comfort of any particular person. Its compassion, if you see it this way, is merciless. It keeps coming at us. It doesn't stop. The compassion is the fact that it doesn't give up on us or coddle us in a sentimental way. It has no respect for our personal judgments or evaluations.

These intelligences are compassionate because they radiate an endless love, but they are not compassionate in the sense of saying, "Let's not give Arthur a hard time today. Let's be nice to him." You can't attach a human judgment.

Individuals open to these forces according to their individual, evolutionary gift. The most public examples are the Mozarts, Shakespeares and Blakes. But each of us has the same kind of access as a potential, but the expression is likely to be different.

What's interesting about those individuals who have come to the earth bearing gifts of that magnitude is that often the access is limited to one particular channel. It isn't integrated into the whole life. There can be great confusion in the personal life because of those forces. Very few geniuses have spoken of their gift as coming from them. They knew that they had broken through a certain door so that something poured through them, even against their conscious will sometimes.

It is possible to enter into a very deep relationship with these forces in an integrated way and not just through certain doors.

Arthur: I feel, with what you are saying, an enormous hope. I had stopped at a place that didn't include the evolutionary perspective. I stopped at what seemed to me to be an advanced psychological perspective which was based on the importance of being seen, heard and acknowledged by somebody else.

You are saying that there is something beyond that perspective.

Yes, but without negating what you just said. There is a need to be acknowledged, to feel someone else and also there is something well beyond that. When someone acknowledges us or we acknowledge someone else, we are bringing certain forces into play through our appreciation. We are a messenger for forces greater than ourselves.

Kathy's struggle, for instance, is taking place on many different levels. Her struggle with the meaning of womanhood, her struggle with the past, her struggle with male/female intimacy, are all real, but it is vital to see that these psychological struggles are taking place at one end of the spectrum. They represent evolutionary movements that are actually occurring on a deeper, energetic level.

Rachael: As you speak of the energies moving through us and the difference between our labels and the actual energy, I was struck by the way I personalize all of that. I'm very curious about that process.

Personalizing, to a certain extent, is inevitable and appropriate. This body is a unique configuration of energetic impulses. The person, which is our conventional sense of self, is a contraction — an inverted globe of memory, belief, conditioning and thought. The true individuality is a pulsation of energy in a specific configuration. But the individuality itself, in a real sense, is a contraction of some greater presence — something more universal. Each aspect of the human being, as we descend from universality to personality, is a narrower passageway.

The creative process is a balanced interplay between vast energies and ever-narrowing passageways. Great energies move into the wide end of a horn and are funneled intensely through it toward the narrow end where they emerge as form — whether that form be an idea, a vision, a warmth in the heart or some concrete act or service.

It is part of our purpose as human beings to individualize cosmic energies, so we must personalize them to some extent. That's part of the fun.

The question becomes whether the individualizing and the personalizing create a loss of relationship to the greater sphere — whether they end up separated from the whole and therefore evoking fear.

Loneliness comes from the perceptual illusion that the personal end of the great horn has an existence which is independent of the wide end of the horn and of the energies which pour through it.

It is because of a perceptual break with ecological interdependence, with the great weave of life, that so much of our suffering begins to arise. This life is a marvelous interplay between form and formlessness, creative energy and narrow passageways, between density and desire.

Rachael: As you speak, I am struck by the difference between personalizing and taking something personally.

Arthur: I've been listening to what you are saying and I'm trying to enter into it in an experiential way. When I think my wife is withdrawing from me and I feel the aloneness, what are you suggesting I do in terms of all that has been said?

When you experience the aloneness, it needs to be acknowledged as a bedrock experience. It's important to see that it has been with you for a long time and that you have understandably avoided being with it directly. You would rather do any number of things other than encounter the aloneness. One way of avoiding that encounter is to let the needs of relationship become a substitute for it.

We go to our aloneness without calling it any name at all. We locate it physically, transcending the mind's absorption with metaphorical stories. We go to it and live with it instead of living against it.

Such an entry into our own experience is a form of self-respect. We don't need any other reason for doing it even though there are many. The moment we think that there is something about us which is foreign or wrong, something we have to get over, then we are not respecting the whole being. We are caught in the fragment.

Loneliness is more than a psycho-physical experience. It is a kind of door. It is a kind of prayer, an opening to something that we have longed for across an entire life. Through hurt or loneliness we can make the passage to what we want. By standing back we can't.

Entering into any feeling experience without the structural demand of thought allows us to know the way in which energy, the Presence, is touching our body. Therefore all feeling experiences must be treated as sacred. We approach them respectfully. We breathe with them. We allow and listen.

Gary: Doesn't this all begin only when we can stop blaming someone else for our pain?

The blaming is an attempt to shift our attention away from pain and toward what we assume to be the cause of that pain. It is always a distraction from a true entry into the greater life.

On the other side of this, though, it is vital to know that if we are blaming someone for our pain, for what we think they have done to us, we can't just jump that place with the idea that there is something greater. We can't skip the stages.

Blaming may be a stage. This must be accepted. We have to be able to look at it and maybe even say "yes" to it. Otherwise we become consumed by moral commandments and abstractions.

Beliefs are not substitutes for actual passages. If we believe, for instance, that it is better not to blame, and we use that belief as a pressure, then it becomes difficult to enter into the open space. It is through working with ourselves in a spirit of complete acceptance that we learn to move through an ordeal such as the obsession of blame.

Gary: In my head I can sort of thank someone for making me angry or sad, but that isn't really caring for myself nor does it get me beyond it.

That's right. The movement doesn't come through fantasy. We can make images, carry beliefs, repeat phrases, but these things don't really shift the perception from isolation to relatedness.

Arthur: Somehow all this must bring a person to the question of what does the blaming really make you feel in yourself? Can the wounded feeling offer us direction?

Yes, the wound has a psychological component, a physical component, a subtle physical component, and a vast spiritual component. It is guidance. It is intelligent communication. It is a message to the one who will listen, and listening means treating the wound as a sacred possibility. Our pain is the congestion, inflammation, rawness in a passageway between dense physical reality and the current of life itself.

The healing that we speak about here is an opening into vulnerability at every step. The body's passageways must open. Only through the body being open in a delicate and vulnerable way can we experience the transcendent light, the love. Our striving is never to get over something, but to get into something.

6

We have become so
intermingled,
so shared, that the
"I love you" or "You love me"
doesn't make sense.
We share a unified field
which is recognized to be love.

Joseph: I have an issue that causes me a lot of pain and I think it has to do with the self-critical voice. It comes about because of a certain kind of thin skin. The main arena is with my wife.

I spoke with her yesterday and when I asked her what she was doing, somehow my questions upset her, and then I became upset myself. I think what I do to myself is think that there is something wrong with me for asking questions that upset her. It breaks the intimacy between us.

What was the nature of the questions that upset her? Did she say?

Joseph: I don't know.

How do you know she was upset?

Joseph: She stopped talking.

Is that a familiar style?

Joseph: Yes.

She never communicated the upset to you. She just stayed silent.

Joseph: I asked her if she was upset and she said yes.

Did she say what it was about the questions that made her upset?

Joseph: She said that my questions indicated to her that I hadn't heard what she had said.

She was saying that you were, in effect, asking her to repeat pieces of information that she had already conveyed.

Joseph: That I kept asking the same questions even though she had answered them, as if I hadn't heard them. To me her answers didn't answer my questions.

When you said that this issue upsets you, do you mean that you became upset with her or with yourself?

Joseph: I felt pain in myself. I felt the pain of being rejected. I'm not sure what it is. I get confused. I think that there is something in me when I act naturally that causes a breakdown in intimacy.

You're saying that the questions you asked in that situation were natural.

Joseph: I was actually very curious. But it came across to her as being demanding in some sense and inappropriate.

Let's allow the attention to be with the body. Breathe easily. I was starting to feel a kind of tangle coming on — not a tangle between you and me, but as if we were going somewhere that didn't make sense. I think there is something very real here and I didn't want it to get lost. So I thought we should just breathe and steady ourselves a little bit.

Joseph: I certainly had a bodily experience when I spoke with her. I felt hurt, disappointment and tension. I feel it again now.

How would you have preferred her to respond? What kind of response would not have evoked that kind of hurt or tension?

Joseph: I was genuinely interested in what she was doing and I wanted to find out what it was.

And she interpreted it differently than that.

Joseph: I suspect that basically it had nothing to do with me.

Does that suspicion change the body response?

Joseph: Not at all.

Because that suspicion is more philosophical than real. No matter what it was that motivated her response to you, you took it in as an attack or a humiliation of one sort or another. It brought you to a belief in your inadequacy. A vulnerable hurt started rising up to the surface.

Joseph: Yeah, it has a huge effect on our relationship because when I feel this way I tend to go away. I don't mean physically. I'm just not there.

You go away for a good period of time or a short period of time?

Joseph: It varies.

But sometimes you do lock yourself away for periods of time.

Joseph: I become distant and unavailable for various periods.

Is the tension you are experiencing now one of the elements in the distancing?

Joseph: Yes.

It's maintained as a kind of wrap, meaning that it is there but you are not conscious of it all the time.

Joseph: I become conscious of it afterwards. It happens very quickly. At some point I become aware of anger, but not in the situation yesterday.

Does this response get you somewhere in the relationship?

Joseph: Of course not.

I don't mean the question in a rhetorical way. It is certainly possible in a relationship that when one of the partners disappears into tightness, it brings the other partner back.

Joseph: It has the opposite effect with us. She feels abandoned.

She gets angry.

Joseph: More alienated.

She doesn't come toward you. She waits until you come out from your own distance.

Joseph: Right, but my real question right now is what do I do with it? I'm trying to become more aware of how I feel in my body, but I'm not sure how well I am doing that.

Do you recognize that the response, the disappearing reflex, is a long term response? It's been with you a large part of your life.

Joseph: Yes.

It's something that is really there, part of your relationship to relationship.

Joseph: It is very much a reflex.

Do you feel that distancing tightness right now?

Joseph: Yes, I do. I don't feel it strongly, but I have felt it ever since I talked with her.

Can you describe in almost a geographical way, where it is, what the terrain is like, etc.?

Joseph: It is sort of a wrapping around the heart area. It is like being bound up with cloth or rope.

You feel that now?

Joseph: Yes.

Let's explore what you feel right now because to explore the memory of your feeling can become very complex. Is the feeling only around your heart or does it extend across your chest?

Joseph: Just around my heart.

Would you describe the front of your body as being predominantly on the warm side, the cool side or neutral?

Joseph: It feels warm.

Where do you feel the warmth? Is it in the upper part of the chest or the solar plexus?

Joseph: It's in the upper part of my chest, just below the neck.

The knot or the band around your heart doesn't share that warmth?

Joseph: The warmth reaches from my neck down into it.

So the band and the warmth coexist at this moment. Is the breathing easy right now or are you holding it a little bit?

Joseph: I'm holding it a little bit.

So let's breathe for a minute. Can you feel your breathing?

Joseph: Yes.

Can you feel it in the front of your body as a whole, or is it localized?

Joseph: It is all up and down.

Can you include the tightness of the heart in the breathing? Does it move and sway with the breathing?

Joseph: I can feel it being moved, but it is all moving like a unit.

Is the warmth part of the unit?

Joseph: Yes.

Let's stay with this. Stay with the body. Stay with the breathing. How does the body feel now?

Joseph: It feels much more open and loose, like the knot is dissolving.

Is there more warmth or is it pretty much the same?

Joseph: There is more and it is going all around my body.

Let's stay with it again. Let the attention be with the heart and the breathing very gently. Stay with it in an easy way. Is it loosening a little more?

Joseph: Yes.

Okay, are your thoughts active or are they relatively still?

Joseph: Pretty still. There's a lot more heat now.

This is a very different heat from heat which would come from an outside source.

Joseph: It seems to be radiating from within. It feels like my whole front area is open.

You mean literally open, don't you?

Joseph: It feels like there is no flesh anymore.

Let's do something with the mind for a minute. Just remember your conversation yesterday. Bring it back into consciousness. Does it affect your body to remember it?

Joseph: It stays generally open. There is a slight closing.

Can you describe the closing?

Joseph: It is as if there were shutters around my abdomen. They close and open.

Let's go to that and experience it directly. Do you feel the heat?

Joseph: It's incredible.

As the body opens like this we have the opportunity to discover love in a new way. Isn't some of the warmth a kind of appreciation for what is happening at this moment?

Joseph: I definitely feel that here. The problem for me is that I lose that sense with my wife.

I understand that. The shuttering reflex is designed to stop this from happening.

Joseph: I think I believe that her acting that way means that she doesn't want to interact with me. I don't want the feelings of love to stop at that.

That's true. That is the way it should be. But right now it is something you are telling yourself in a theoretical way.

Joseph: My closing down is so powerful.

Can you see, as we sit here, that closing the shutters in the way you do with her is closing this — the warmth, the open front?

Joseph: Yes.

There is something more here. Let's stay looking at the space we are in. Do you feel space?

Joseph: Right now I feel so much space that it seems like there is a playing field between us.

The playing field between us connects us and is alive. It is not empty space. Something alive between us is passing the verbal communication. In a spatial sense, do you feel me to be far away or close?

Joseph: I feel close.

Do you feel warmly towards me?

Joseph: Yes.

I feel warmly towards you. It feels good.

Joseph: I almost feel a kind of oneness.

The body is literally thrown open, and something unified rather than divisive arises from that opening. Our bodies are still separate, but they don't contain us anymore so we don't feel isolated, disengaged.

Here is a living example of what is meant by "there is no space between us." Also you can see that when we close the shutters, we become isolated and contained. We become an entity apart from others. When the shutters are thrown open, we are no longer someone like we were before. We are no longer contained within the boundaries of the body and so we can experience what is called love.

The reason we can experience love like this is because there is no separate "other" to love. When we find ourselves contained within the cage of the body, love can not be experienced in this way. Love is truly available when the walls of separation begin to fall apart.

When someone hurts us, it can become a reminder to the separated egoic identity that we must protect ourselves against the existence of another. We close the body back into a cage and lurk in our separate space.

We can observe how closing in this way represents a different use of the body from the way you and I are using our bodies right now. It is the opposite. To protect ourselves, we close the cage, and the experience of being alone is distinct. It is hard to return because there appear to be so many reasons to stand away and protect ourselves.

You and I are experiencing the way in which the body can become like a window. It is flung open in a certain way. The beauty of a situation like this is that we are able to verbalize even while the body's window is open. This open window changes the whole dimensional sense of space in relationship.

I can say that I love you, but that's not really it. That's an approximation. I can say that I feel your love, but that's not it either. We have become so intermingled, so shared, that the "I love you" or "You love me" doesn't make sense. We share a unified field which is recognized to be love.

Do you still feel it?

Joseph: Yes.

It's not vague. It's a very real experience, isn't it?

Joseph: Very real.

Someone might say that it is all well and good to have this experience here, but I can't have it with my wife very much, especially when we enter into certain kinds of reactions. While this may be true right now, we are exercising a way of using the body which must be repeatedly practiced before we can remain open in the face of an encounter which so accentuates our sense of aloneness.

In the psychological terrain, the suggestion would be that the issue is located at that particular interaction with your wife or at other interactions like it. Here we are saying that the issue which you have brought forward in relationship to your wife is related to a reflex of the body. The psychological end is only an expression, a symbol of the bodily experience.

To find a place or a way to practice opening the body and to maintain that opening during verbal communication is assisting in working with the localized outcroppings of what you called the issue. We are showing the body a different response from what it has been taught in the past. We are turning the other cheek. We are not flexing into contraction. We are melting into expansion.

Do you feel afraid of me as we sit?

Joseph: No.

I don't feel afraid of you either because no otherness really exists here. A boundary exists but it is more like a window frame. We know we have a body. It is able to encounter this exchange as a kind of erotic resonance. This is the value of the body. It can consciously experience oneness. It is a paradox. The body, which is a symbol of our apparent separation, is the only vehicle that can actually feel the effects of love, of unity.

Joseph: The way to practice dealing with this is to return to the body and be with the pain as it is?

It is very important for you to notice the entire aesthetic dimension of the pain. Notice where it is, how it feels, what it's doing to the physical frame. Explore it, but don't mystify it or make it a source of shame. And in the exploration allow the feeling to change. It shouldn't be tied down to what it seems to be at the beginning of the exploration.

We can't explore pain harshly. It must be explored warmly because the exploration itself is a stimulus for the body to open. The pain is contraction and it is unnatural because the function of the body is to be a window with the sash drawn and the glass clean.

The pain is a signal of contraction. It is not a signal of wrongness. We explore the pain because the pain itself is just a tightened version of what you and I are experiencing right now.

It may be helpful to apply physical, external warmth to the pain, like the palms of your hands or even a hot water bottle. You may want to put something on the front of the body which is comforting. Or you can just stay with it and experience it as a work of art and not as a moral dilemma or a psychological difficulty.

Always remember to stay with your breathing. It is important to breathe rhythmically. If you find yourself caught in the mire of thought, come back to the breathing.

It is also important as you do this to witness compassionately what you are saying to yourself about the pain — how you are dealing with it from the conceptual frame, how you are trying to explain, to demean and attack. Just notice that. If you blame your wife, yourself or your past, don't try to do anything about it.

None of this is complex. It is all warm observation. Notice experientially the relationship between what you are saying to yourself, in terms of its physical location, where the feeling is coming from. Where is the voice and where is the pain? We can even rock back and forth between the two. This process of rocking back and forth between where the pain is and where the concept is has real value. All this takes steady breathing and a warm detachment. You can come to a point where what the mind says does not grip you in the way it did before.

Going to the head is a serious disruption of the rhythm of the body, the breathing and of the pulsation of love itself. We restore balance and health by inducing rhythm. We rock back and forth between the mental frame and the body while we breathe consciously. After a while the content loses its magnetism. As we breathe and rock on the subtle physical level, we may even choose to lightly rock the body — to breathe and rock and allow.

So much of our work with what we might call neurotic process is a work with space, rhythm and movement. Every neurosis which arises from contraction is accompanied by a loss of rhythm and space. Rhythm and space become oppressed by the rigidity of the body and the arrhythmic sequence of thought. To stimulate rhythm in the body is to begin a return to the restoration that we seek.

It is important that you are not engaging in these practices because something is wrong with you. This work is not about getting over something in any traditional sense. The contraction and the expansion are the same thing appearing in different ways. There is nothing wrong with the window because the shades are closed. It's just that we can't see out at that time. When the shades are lifted, it is the same window, only now the light has come, the wider view is available.

Our life is a dance of rhythm, warmth, movement and space, and it is to these qualities that we return when attempting to restore a sense of grace to our experience.

These simple practices are organic and gentle. They are not techniques in the usual sense. They represent a way of relating to our own individual existence which is based on the compassionate understanding that life is innocent and, therefore, we have nothing to be afraid of.

Right now I am speaking to your open body and not to your mind. Something is being exchanged which is different from information. It penetrates like a wave of warmth and resides within like a seed ready to sprout. You can always find this again. It may take more time without the attentive intermingling of two hearts. But it is yours and it can be done.

What is your experience right now?

Joseph: I feel an incredible energetic connection between us. The heat is more in my body and concentrated around the heart.

An actual work is going on right now in your body. It is important that we stay with it gently in the silence.

7

A deep relationship
with someone else is impossible
as long as
we are terrified of ourselves.

Joan: I wish I had come here last week, because right now I'm on an external high. Everything is going my way so I'm thinking, why am I here?

You certainly don't have to be feeling any particular way to move closer to yourself. As you talk about this high can you describe to me what it feels like in a bodily sense?

Joan: In a bodily sense, it's almost like a fluttery feeling. Like I can't really catch my breath. I can't sit still. I've got to twiddle my thumbs or chew gum. I've got to do something.

Is that uncomfortable or comfortable?

Joan: Well it's comfortable in the sense that it's a nice distraction. I don't know what it would be like to sit still.

What is the risk in sitting still?

Joan: I feel like I would explode or something.

That's interesting because there's obviously a lot of energy pulsating through your body. You are also having trouble letting it come into the body in a full way. You are actually depleting it through the itchy activity.

We all tend to do that but it would be useful to let that energy rise so that you can really be fed by it. In a sense, you are knocking the energy out at a lower level than it would naturally go to. It is seeking to feed you and then to create. Instead of letting that happen, static is being discharged in various places through restless movement and distractions.

If you could really take in the charge and get it moving up, there is great power in it. Thoughts become clearer. Actions become bolder, etc. The circuitry is filled.

Joan: Even if that energy is coming from kind of an addictive place?

How do you know it's coming from kind of an addictive place?

Joan: Because it's just external circumstances that caused it.

Because things are going well.

Joan: Yeah.

Whether it is because circumstances are going well or for some other reason, the fact is you are having a bodily experience. Energy is pulsating in you. You are shuttering it — that is — dampening it and then letting it free in very short cycles.

It doesn't matter what the cause of it is. You are having an experience with energy that feels like a kind of high.

When you say addictive, I guess you mean that you have let external circumstances make you happy.

Joan: Yes.

That may only be partially true though. You have let yourself become open because things are going well. As a result of this opening, a movement can occur. You want the movement, but you also distrust it. To label all this addictive is to misunderstand the deeper nature of what's going on.

There may certainly be truth in what you are saying, but it may not be an overall truth. There is something else happening besides the mind's addictive patterns.

You are having a movement of creative energies. It may be that the mind is gluing those energies onto the outside in an addictive way. But ultimately you have to learn how to get that energy to charge you and to strengthen you so that the mind's patterns can be broken.

Do you follow me? I don't want to lose you.

Joan: I guess I follow you. I guess I've learned over the past years to look at things as either good or bad. Do you know what I mean?

Exactly, and that's a mental trap. It's an interpretive trap. You don't really know. You know only what you are telling yourself.

The only way you can really know something is to observe it without prejudice. You can't know it on the basis of judgment. I don't mean to throw out something that is meaningful to you, but in the process of growth we must look at the way we are defining our life experience.

The addiction can only cease when, on a deep, subtle level, you stop starving yourself. People starve themselves because they do not know how to deal with basic life energy as it passes through the body.

If a person is suppressing their life energy or depleting it in various ways, they are going to feel a lot of emptiness, a lot of hunger in that sense. The mind interprets that hunger as a need for something on the outside. As we learn how to use the current of energy which passes through us in a deeply nurturing way, some of that starvation ends. So does the addiction.

Dealing with the starvation requires that we dismantle the present interpretation and come to the body and all its subtle aspects in a healing way.

Joan: What do you mean by life energy?

We do not live by bread alone. What sustains the human being is not simply the food we eat. There are energies streaming into us which are subtler than the energies we derive from food.

There are currents of energy pouring toward and into our bodies all the time. The creative faculties are dependent on how we take these currents into ourselves.

Feelings are conscious experiences of energy. They seem like emotions, very personalized, because the mind begins to evaluate them in distinctly clutching ways. When we loosen up the domination of the mind's clutch, the emotions become various movements of energy in the body. They are unique movements, but they are not loaded with personal meaning. How we deal with these energies, these feelings, is critical to our sense of well-being here on the earth.

All this may sound wild to you or it may sound great. In either case it's interesting to explore.

Most of us perceive the body to be a container. We sit inside that container and try to survive. We conceive of ourselves to be some thoughts, beliefs, memories, emotions, etc.

As we gain a deeper view, we can experience the body as a kind of membrane which is constantly receiving and giving currents of energy. These energies make up our feeling life, our creative life and our relationship with each other. We've been taught very little about what to do with these energies. Your agitation or nervousness is a steam-off of these energies instead of letting them flood you.

Joan: How would I let them flood me? By just sitting still?

Not necessarily. First it is important for you to observe this — that you take a clear look at what's going on. It is important to observe your experience right now in physical terms. Watch the way you tighten and loosen. When the energy builds up and is blocked off, there is a push to do things, to move.

Without becoming passive, but for periods of time, it is good to breathe with it, allow it, without doing anything about it. Such an activity makes you stronger. The energies in the body seek to arise and expand. They feed you. You are in a struggle with that expansion and therefore the nourishing can not take place.

Joan: It sounds so simple, but it doesn't take into account that you are not always going to be on your own side. What about the time when you are against yourself, like a sabotage?

Yes, it is very simple. It also is not easy. There is a huge distinction there. So many of us have the habit of turning against ourselves over and over again.

The habit gets broken by catching ourselves when the self-hatred begins and looking for the bodily experience underneath. We stay with that and breathe. The thoughts may run wild. We may even succumb to them, but when we are ready, we just come back to the body. If we do enter into a cycle of self-hate, it must not be treated as a failure, but as part of a long term process that has an ebb and flow.

There is a significant choice here. Each of us has been taught to treat the evolutionary process in a primitive way. And now, we are learning how to be delicate with what is actually going on. It takes time. At first we wait for those moments when we are conscious of entering into the habitual cycle, and we begin to transcend it. Later it becomes more automatic.

Joan: I'm feeling sort of panicky right now. Everything on the outside I wanted is working out, but now it doesn't feel like enough. It's scary.

It isn't enough. You are right. It's great and good for you, but in and of itself, there is no real fulfillment.

Joan: Now I feel so shallow and superficial for being happy about my success.

Now that is sabotage. That's an attack on yourself. You have every right to feel happy about it. It is one of the joys of life to see things work out. It's lovely to feel good when you have an achievement. It is even lovelier to stay at ease and open when things don't seem to be working out, to stay caring.

But you see, if you can't do it when something "good" is happening, it is very difficult to do it when something "bad" is happening.

Joan: I kind of bounce back and forth between the happiness and something else — a low. I know it helps to just go with it, but also I'm afraid if I do that, then I really get stuck in it forever.

When you are low or depressed there is a way of allowing yourself to experience it, not as a mental state, but as a distinct physical state. You can physicalize the low or the depression. Just let yourself feel the vulnerability, the sadness, the rawness, and as you do that it changes in character. It's different.

If you stay with the thoughts and the heavy feeling as if they were the same, it becomes a kind of indulgence which doesn't lead you to the place where you want to go. By physicalizing, breathing, allowing the feeling to exist, you can be let out of it.

Joan: But how do you physicalize it?

A depression or low has three elements to it: what you are telling yourself in the mind, consciously and unconsciously, a heavy close-down of the physical body and something underneath that which is at the core and needs to be discovered.

These three elements sit in a pile causing what is termed a depression. To physicalize it means to not pay as much attention to the mental aspect and then to let yourself sink into the physical experience. You come to the close-down, the tension, first and then something much subtler occurs.

The thought level of a depression is not the most interesting aspect of it. The depression also can not be solved on that level. It's the habit part. The deep physical level, the feeling level, is the most interesting part. But it is not what you think it is. It's different. Given the slightest opening, the depression can shift. It can move.

Joan: I think I understand what you are saying. Can I feed it back?

Yes, please.

Joan: I know this is true for myself. The mind becomes a trap after a while. It's almost tiring. You wish you could turn it off.

When I get really depressed my thoughts are always the same. There is nothing new in them at all. There is nothing dramatic or exciting. It's all old stuff. There are no answers in what new way I can hurt myself. It all seems the same, but just to go into a state where the mind is turned off.

I agree. The thoughts you are having during a depression are nothing but habits. They are boring. The close-down of the body, the sense of heaviness, is also a habit.

What's not a habit is something which is happening underneath that both the thoughts and the gross physical close-down are trying to protect against —something more delicate, more vulnerable and moving, something at the edge of conceptual safety.

Joan: What is that?

You have to discover it to really know. There is no name for it. But it is a beautiful part of you. I'm not trying to avoid answering you by suggesting that I know something you don't. I am saying that this discovery is so experiential, so subtle, so intimate to us that we can only talk about it poetically.

The depression is an assault on an energetic movement. That movement, at base, has a creative capacity. But it may be experienced, at the beginning, as being very vulnerable, delicate and raw depending on how we have dealt with it in the past.

There is much more to you than your thoughts and your depression. There is an entire relationship to life which is occurring on the level of energy. Coming into contact with it changes your experience. It takes discipline and willingness.

Joan: Once you have that experience, do you lose the fear of it?

You start to. Once you have allowed yourself to do it, and this happens over time, the fear diminishes.

How do you experience yourself right now? Can you describe your experience right now expressively, not mechanically?

Joan: It's difficult because I don't feel very here most of the time. I'm in the past or the future. I have a little nausea. It's almost like there is a small thread running through my body from top to bottom. It's very sensitive. I feel like I must wrap it in something. The thread is very sensitive.

Can you put your attention directly on that thread without tightening your breathing?

Joan: Yes.

Also notice when you go into thought.

Joan: (Silence) What should I be noticing about it?

Absolutely nothing. Just notice it. There is no goal. When you say, "What should I notice about it?" it almost means, "What should I do about it?" or, "What's the point?" The purpose is to be with yourself rather than fighting yourself — to be in a more attentive position.

Joan: For me to be attentive is to be frightened.

I hear what you are saying. When you are attentive like that you get frightened. The attention and the fear are not the same, however. When you come to yourself directly, you get frightened.

Joan: Yes.

Then notice that experience. You have this thread running down through you. You come to it openly and then you get frightened.
 How do you know you're frightened? What are the symptoms?

Joan: I just feel very uncomfortable.

Is it bad to be uncomfortable?

Joan: Yes.

Why?

Joan: I don't know why. It just is.

You've been taught to distract yourself when there is discomfort. This goes against the rules.

Joan: Right.

You are now shoving your face in it. Look at the discomfort, feel it. There is no way around it. You must go through yourself. If you are always running away, there must be a turn toward some addictive solution.

If you have a discomfort about some feeling and you always distract yourself from it, if you do something about it instead of for it, then you're saying that there is something wrong with you. There is a foreignness in you. You've got to stay away from it. What I'm saying is that you need to go to yourself instead of fighting against yourself, even if it is very painful.

A deep relationship with someone else is impossible as long as we are terrified of ourselves. Intimate relationship pulls everything out and there will have to be some sort of protective dependency and some sort of defending. We will have to use the other person to keep away from ourselves.

On the other hand, if you turn toward yourself even when it's rough, even when you would rather be doing anything else, you become a fearless person. You become able to step forward fearlessly.

Joan: Even if your first instinct is to sabotage it.

Yes, because it is not an instinct. It's a habit, a part of your conditioning. It's a teaching every one of us has received to one degree or another. Our unhappiness, our discomfort are enemies. Our happiness, our comfort are friends. We are taught to do anything we can to avoid the enemy so that we can always have the friend. But it doesn't work. As long as you are struggling with yourself, you can't find the happiness. The reasons you bobble around from past to future and have a hard time being here in the present is because you see your discomfort as an enemy.

Do you follow me?

Joan: I should just sit with it, always?

At first we sit with it. Later we can live and go about our activities being open to ourselves in this way. It doesn't mean that we always have to sit.

There are many times when a person can feel sad or even angry and go about their daily activities in a simple way.

Joan: Not trying to change anything.

Exactly, the whole body is in a continual pulsation. You breathe; your heart beats; the blood moves through the veins. On gross and subtle levels there is a constant movement. Digestion is a movement. Elimination is a movement. All life is rhythm and movement. Feelings are also movement.

When we have a hypnotic suggestion attached to a feeling and we use the body to tighten down on the feeling because we have assigned it a particular label, movement is arrested. Something is held back that seeks movement and flow.

The journey is to get the feeling moving again. We breathe with it. We allow it. We attend to it. We don't get stuck in the interpretation and we certainly don't try to change it or make it a better feeling. It will change on its own.

Do you still feel aggravated?

Joan: No, I don't. I feel a lot of okayness. I feel that what we talk about here addresses core things but not in terms of the dynamics — inner child or anything like that. This is about the most basic things. Nothing could get any closer. Nothing else gets me closer.

It is so intimate that it doesn't seem to have a content anymore in the usual sense. It's not about your childhood or anything like that. It's about your relationship to life itself.

8

Why would we deliberately choose
to know nothing,
to long for love honestly,
and to confess our neediness?

Human beings develop like plants. We unfold organically. The flower is the front of the body, the frontal membrane. In childhood that membrane opens in a totally vulnerable way. It is so delicate, so easily injured. Some of us have received messages in various forms which suggest that it is safer to close down, not to bloom.

The central message of Compassionate Self-Care is that in order to enter the Kingdom of Heaven we must become like children again. We must return to the flowered state of childhood without sacrificing the integrated strength of our adult development. Innocence must return to our frontal experience.

Kaye: That idea scares me to death.

You're in a different place, Kaye, from this morning. Your expression has a different quality to it now. I understand the fear. Why would we want to embark on a journey like this? Why would we deliberately choose to be vulnerable, to know nothing, to long for love honestly and to confess our neediness?

There is something enormously attractive about the work we do here. It has the lure of the forbidden and the fear as well. Sometimes after opening in the way you did this morning, there might be a sense of remorse. We wonder why we opened up like that. We might think that we made a fool of ourselves. What was that about?

This morning you opened deeply. You were on the edge and began to fall. After lunch, life seems a little more sober. You question yourself and the safety of all this. A quiet paranoia has emerged.

We open like children and then become afraid. We assume, as we did at a certain point in childhood, that it is safer to close down, that we must protect ourselves. We replay over and over again our childhood experience at a subtle and gross bodily level. We are engaged here in a profoundly spiritual work because we are allowing ourselves to experience our own neediness. We are respecting the prayer. The spiritual path is not a superficial affirmation of wholeness. It is a recognition and an experiential affirmation of our neediness. One does not come to a so-called state of wholeness by trying to bypass neediness. We must go through it, dignify it and find what we really need on this earth, what we are longing for.

Maria, how do you feel sitting here? What has your day been like?

Maria: I've been dealing with my familiar pattern. When you were doing the initial meditation this afternoon, I thought, "What is this, mass hypnosis?" Every time you spoke, I would go deeper in spite of my commentary, but the commentary would continue on.

What is the familiar part of that commentary? I know the specifics of this situation may not be familiar, but what is the familiar part of the commentary for you, distrust?

Maria: Yeah, as I get into a space of more openness, and I experience the love more directly, it feels dangerous. I start experiencing fear and then I start following that. At that point, any commentary will do. It doesn't matter what the words are, as long as I get out of that space.

What is the belief suggesting about love or the deeper space?

Maria: You mean where it came from?

No, what do you feel will happen to you if you let yourself fall into love?

Maria: Obliteration — that I would go away somewhere and not come back.

Yes, yes, it's like melting away. Isn't that what you're saying?

Maria: Yeah.

The way that you know yourself now will actually disappear. You will go away in a certain sense. That's part of the work.

Maria: As you were speaking I began to experience planes of energy instead of you and everyone else. It terrified me so much that I fell asleep.

Right before you fell asleep you were experiencing a level of intimacy on the energetic level. Is that what frightened you?

Maria: Yes, very much. And you see, I came hoping for that very experience. I was on a roller coaster, being with my feelings and then going away.

On another level, you wanted that intimacy. You were hoping for it and had created a mental expectation. Do you know what I'm saying? You really want this connection; you want something to happen. A high anticipation dominates. And maybe it happens and maybe it doesn't. In general, that kind of expectation or anticipation is a block, a veiled sabotage. The intimacy, the connection is stopped. When the intimacy, the spaciousness, began to spontaneously arise, you didn't have a defense up. You felt it strongly and then went to sleep.

Maria: I was actually hearing almost all of what you said and it spoke to me directly. And so even though I was sort of asleep, somehow I was hearing a lot of what was going on.

Where do you find yourself right now?

Maria: I feel the deep silence in the room. It makes me want to cry. And I'm also aware of a pain in my gut, the tightness, a very familiar pain.

How open are you to it right now? I get the sense that you're distancing yourself from it a little bit.

Maria: I'm right in the middle of it now.

Where is the pain? Is it literally in your gut?

Maria: Kind of lower bowel, left side.

It's a tightness, or a sense of mass, or....

Maria: It's a weight.

And how does that weight manifest itself in your life? Does it become emotional at certain times, like a heaviness or a sadness?

Maria: It becomes any kind of emotion you can imagine, from sadness to panic to tremendous energy and joy.

But when the energy and joy are there, is the feeling of density or heaviness lessened? Is it less congested?

Maria: Yeah, the congestion has for the moment dissipated.

But sometimes that sensation is translated into other emotions — panic, sadness, joy, whatever it is. But right now, the way I'm hearing you, it hasn't become an emotion. It's just there. Is that true?

Maria: Right now, yeah. It's weight.

You couldn't name it as an emotion right now. It's just weight. I'm not asking you to name it, I'm trying to understand what you are expressing.

Maria: I'm trying to feel what's there. It's weight unless I relax it a little bit, or stop holding against it and then it becomes...actually, it becomes terror. It's a very strong fear.

Are you saying that if you don't maintain a certain level of control, terror comes — that you must keep this feeling at a certain level of density, otherwise it becomes fear?

Maria: Yes.

How close are you right now to the terror?

Maria: Very close.

Do you want to go any closer or would you rather not?

Maria: I don't feel reluctant because it seems like the whole universe is standing around me, waiting for me.

That's beautiful, but....

Maria: But for some reason I just can't be there.

Is it an exploding terror? Does it want to expand and expand, or is it a contracting terror? Do you know what I mean?

Maria: I do. It's a contracting terror actually.

Okay, now let's just go to it. Let's feel it in the body. Let's go to it and breathe with it.

Maria: It almost has a rhythm.

That's interesting. What kind of rhythm, pulsing?

Maria: Yeah, if I contract down on it, it becomes really painful everywhere in my body. It can breathe in a way, and when I let it go, for instance, I'm aware of it in the present. Then it's safe again because I'm also aware of the love in the room. And then it comes back down and squeezes again.

Can you relax into it right now, enough to find the rhythm, how it wants to breathe?

Maria: Yeah.

Can you breathe with it in just the way it wants to breathe?

Maria: (Breathing)

That's great. Stay with that. I'm here with you. Just stay with it. Keep going. Keep going with it....Is there a scream somewhere in the background?

Maria: There probably could be. There has been before.

Just keep going with the breathing. Stay with the breathing....What is the feeling experience right now, Maria?

Maria: I'm electrified.

You mean you're vibrating. Do you know I'm with you?

Maria: Yes.

Now let the attention be with your body. Is there a sense of heaviness there, like before?

Maria: No, it moved to my upper body which feels like it needs a breaking open, you know.

Let's go to it in the upper body. Does it still want to breathe in the upper body? Is it seeking to breathe?

Maria: No, actually it's not. It's seeking a way to open. It doesn't know how to open.

It wants to open.

Maria: Yes.

Where in the upper body do you experience this most intensely — the wanting to break open?

Maria: In my heart area. It's strange because it's almost as though there are hands going from my heart to my ears. Even my face and chest want to open.

Everything wants to open. Do you feel frustrated because it's not opening?

Maria: There's a frustration.

Can you come to your heart right now? Can you be with your heart?

Maria: Yes.

Can you also allow your attention to be with me through your heart?

Maria: Yeah, I feel you.

Don't let your thoughts get into this. Just stay with it. Do you feel me? Do you love me?

Maria: Yes, very much.

Is that safe?

Maria: Well, I'm not terrified. I'm just shy.

Yes, and the shyness is a kind of contraction, or is it a kind of innocence?

Maria: I guess the fear of being seen.

Yeah. There's a child in this too, isn't there? I mean in this shyness, in this openness, in this fear of being seen. You know what I mean? Like a way you were, some memory.

Maria: Yeah, yes.

Is there any memory in this at all, Maria? Does anything come up for you?

Maria: About this face?

Yes, about this face, about this shyness, the love, the feeling of love. I'm not asking you to dig. I'm just wondering if something comes, a dream, a memory.

Maria: Well, actually I've been in this space a lot. As a kid, I was in this space a lot.

And when you say this space, you mean the love?

Maria: The love.

When you say you were in this a lot, is there an "and" to that or is that it?

Maria: Well, then I was also afraid of what would happen after I was in this space for a while. It was like going toward physical death.

And that's a real fear, the obliteration that death seems to bring. Where is death for you in a personal sense? Have you been near death in your life?

Maria: Yes, I've almost died more than once.

In what circumstances do you remember that happening? What is the strongest memory?

Maria: (Silence) Well, unfortunately, I was hung.

You were hung in what way? Somebody hung you?

Maria: Somebody hung me.

And who was that somebody?

Maria: My dad.

And how did you release yourself from that?

Maria: I had a near-death experience and then he cut me down.

And what was the nature of the near-death experience?

Maria: The roof came off the room I was in and light was above me and love was there.

And for him as well?

Maria: I don't know.

It was just there.

Maria: It was there.

And at the time that he did that to you, did you know why he was doing it? Was it completely irrational or was there some explanation, however strange, for him doing it?

Maria: He was crazy.

Yeah, does that worry you?

Maria: Yeah.

I mean are you afraid somehow that in going to this space that a craziness could come upon you?

Maria: Yes.

And how does that fear take a specific form, Maria? What are you afraid of, how would you go crazy?

Maria: I would lose my mind and become psychotic and out of touch.

Does that happen to you periodically?

Maria: No.

Does it not happen to you, do you think, because you control yourself or because it's simply not there?

Maria: I don't think it's there.

It doesn't feel that way to me either. That's not my sense of you at all. I would imagine that you have a flash point, but that's different from breaking with reality. I mean isn't that true, that you have strong flashes of anger?

Maria: Yeah, it's definitely there.

So when the roof opened and there was this light, you felt the love of God or whatever it was?

Maria: Yeah, and telling me, saying that it wasn't my time to die, that they would be with me.

How old were you at that point?

Maria: Nine or ten.

Let's go back to the body again. Let's go to the body. Do you feel love or fear or both?

Maria: I feel no fear at all.

Let's be with each other in a very direct way right now, Maria. Just front to front like this. Do you feel me?

Maria: I feel you almost as a caress. On my head.

And do you feel open? Do you feel spacious to some extent?

Maria: Yes.

Yes, I feel you as space right now. It seems to me that you have come to something, some relationship with yourself that's bigger than it was just a while ago. As you go back to that child, is there a feeling sense of how that child was? I don't mean a visual memory, but a kind of feeling memory of the child, of how she experienced the world?

Maria: Yeah, she was very, very open.

Innocent?

Maria: Yeah, kind of foreign.

But you loved your father?

Maria: Yeah.

It's so beautiful. I'm wondering if you can feel, even in the midst of that painful memory, the exquisite and innocent beauty of loving your father?

Maria: Yeah.

This says something about you. Do you know what I mean? It says something about who you are, about an aspect of you that is the very opposite of psychotic. Do you know what I'm saying?

Maria: Yeah.

There's something incredible about you. Your gift is right here. I can feel what you are.

Maria: It's very hard, after something like what I've experienced. You have certain beliefs and it's just hard.

But when you say "certain beliefs," what are you referring to specifically?

Maria: Saying ....

About the fact that it happened to you?

Maria: Yes.

Are you feeling that right now?

Maria: I'm a little embarrassed.

That this event happened to you?

Maria: No, that I disclosed it, that I disclosed it in the circle.

I'm curious about that. You mean it makes you less of a person to have had that experience, or that people won't like you as much? What is the belief?

Maria: I'm exposing ugliness.

But is it ugly that the roof opened and the angels spoke to you in the midst of a very difficult situation? Is that really an ugliness?

Maria: No.

Is it necessarily an ugliness that as a child you experienced such a challenge, such a painful and difficult challenge? Is that an ugliness?

Maria: Well, I believed that it was ugly.

I hear that, but looking back right now, is there space between the belief that it's ugly and something else, some innocence in relationship to it? Is there a space to question whether it's really ugly or not?

Maria: Well, there's a knowledge that it really isn't ugly.

Is that a real knowledge?

Maria: Yeah.

Can you look at yourself just as you were doing before and feel a beauty?

Maria: Yes.

And can you look at that child and feel the same beauty?

Maria: Yes.

The contrast between a father doing that to you and your living beauty. There is something here which is very deep, something about innocence and the fire of persecution — about standing for something. Deep in this situation is a replica of something ancient, an echo of something that wasn't ugly at all — that was actually a nobility, a quality of courage, even a steadfastness in the face of danger. Do you find that quality in yourself, Maria?

Maria: I do, and for some reason I am reluctant to admit it.

But it is you, isn't it, in a way?

Maria: Yes.

An innocent courage.

Maria: Yes.

Where is the hesitation? I feel it now. There's something so powerful here for you. Is the reluctance also the shame to say something about yourself that's beautiful?

Maria: Yes.

Let's ventilate the belief. What happens if you allow yourself to express what you are? What happens? What happens to someone who allows themselves to be what they are? What happens to you?

Maria: I will be punished.

There is a beautiful interplay here. There's the child with an innocent openness, with these eyes. That's what I see, a flower in the front of the body. Then there's this, what might be called at a certain level, a kind of persecution of that innocence. You opened to the light at a time of severe challenge. And now here also, as an adult, carrying the shame, carrying a fear which suggests that if you reveal what you are, then you will be persecuted again. You will be punished.

The light that came to you that day, the voices which told you that it was not time for you to die are here again. It is time to acknowledge who you are and what you have withstood in this life. It is time to reclaim the willingness and the courage of that child. Do you know what I mean?

Maria: Yeah.

To find that again, and not to be afraid.

Maria: Yes, yes, it's sort of saying it's time to wear that "Wow."

And you can feel the message, can't you?

We can look at our present life and assume, for instance, that we had other lives before it. This is a linear and rather surface-level view of what is going on. This life has many levels. We are not just what we see here. The persecution, the relationship to light runs very deep. Something speaks from these images, something from a deeper, more subtle dimension, something that is part of you. It's a little like Daniel in the lion's den, or the stories in which the persecuted children sing praises to God as they burn in the fire.

It is time for you to reclaim something and to know that nothing like that event ever has to come into your life again. Does this sound strange to you?

Maria: No.

I feel your innocence, and your attractiveness. Is that strange?

Maria: No.

And beyond that, I feel such a love, really such a love, as I sit here in front of you. Can you accept that?

Maria: Yes, I can. I feel not only such a love, but for some reason I've been unburdened. I'm not really sure how, but the opening I was looking for has come. And I'm really thankful.

Is there any anxiety or do you feel clear?

Maria: I feel clear and I feel completely grateful.

Let's all sit together in the silence for a few minutes, all of us, together.

9

We can use content to transcend content.

Denise: I feel that there are so many people to love so why am I going home to live with a man who doesn't care about me and doesn't want me there? Why am I in another relationship with somebody who doesn't love me? But I know that I'm going to go back and do the same thing.

Right.

Denise: No, nothing has changed and I have a great fear of being alone. I feel so afraid to be alone. I've never been alone and, you know, I always want to fix things and I know, you know, that whatever God wills will be done, but I don't know how to solve problems. I have a very big problem with my in-laws. They decided a few months ago that my daughter wasn't really sick and she didn't visit at Christmas and we forgot to call Daddy on his birthday, so we won't send Louise a card on her birthday. And these are people we saw twice a year for twenty years and it was sort of a cordial meeting. And now Father's Day, my husband called to invite them over and his mother said that she was tired of making believe we're a happy family —— just send Daddy a card. So I know this hurt my husband very much.

And it seems like he lost everybody who ever cared for him —— his real parents, his adoptive parents now, and his first wife, you know, and his son. So it seems like he had so many losses. And I wrote them a very nice letter, and that I hoped they call, and how can I buy a Father's Day card saying Happy Father's Day *to someone who never wants to see the family again? And my husband is very hurt and what do I tell my daughter? And I told them I'd like them to call on Father's Day, that I'd like to hear from them. And they didn't respond. And I said, "Okay, that's it. He's not meant to have parents. It's over."*

But at the beginning of this week I kept thinking about it and I know it is bothering me. I know I can't do anything more and I feel I should do something. And I don't know how to take this away to other relationships. I mean I don't have anybody to go home to that I can sit and feel with or communicate with. So, you know, I feel I want to go away and get an apartment somewhere, but I'm afraid to be alone. So, I know I'm going to just stay the way I am. And I guess I feel helpless. I feel very helpless.

I'm with you. I'm just going to sit for a minute. Now let me ask you a serious question, although it may sound like a relatively unrelated question or it may sound like I'm being unsympathetic, but it's a real question. What would you like from me? In other words, in relationship to what you just asked, what would you like from me? On what level are you looking for an answer, Denise? I ask this in total friendship and support. I want to understand what you're really asking.

Denise: I want to know how, when I go home, I can reach out to other people. How can I reach my in-laws? How can you just have family that decides they don't ever want to see you again? I haven't seen them in six months and now that I'm all-loving, I know that if I saw them it would be more positive, but I'm afraid to even pick up the phone. I can't call, not after the letter.

Now let me ask you another question. I'm just kind of feeling my way through this. As you are speaking like this, do you feel that you are speaking with me or are you just speaking? Are you connecting with me? What is your internal experience of the relationship between you and me?

Denise: Well, right now I feel closer than....

Than when you started?

Denise: Yes.

Right now, meaning since I asked that question?

Denise: Yes.

That is, you noticed that you weren't relating to me before my question and then you moved closer. Is that what you're saying?

Denise: Yeah, I think I was speaking in the air.

You see I felt a little disconnected from you and I felt that you were speaking to yourself. It wasn't clear what you wanted from me, if you didn't actually want to speak with me. The question that went through my mind was, "I wonder what Denise wants since she's not speaking to me? I wonder what she's looking for?"

Were you trying to reach out to me? Were you feeling lonely and calling out in some way, but not quite able to do it?

Denise: I'm not feeling lonely right now. I feel that I want to know how to take away what I'm feeling.

And you're feeling what? I'm very interested. What is it you're feeling?

Denise: I'm feeling something in the front of my body.

You're feeling alive?

Denise: I'm feeling vibrations of love.

Yes.

Denise: I wish I could feel this when I get home and am alone. And I guess I want to make my husband feel better. I want to give him his parents back.

That's something you seriously want to do or that's something you're saying you're trying to do?

Denise: I seriously want to do that. I took him to my mother's house two weeks ago thinking, well, that at least he'd have my parents. And my mother treated him just awful. And I felt so bad, now he can never see my parents. But then I thought that maybe this is better. I thought, "If you don't have his parents, then when you leave him you won't have to explain to them, and if you do leave him, you don't have to explain to your mother because she doesn't like him anyway."

So what you were saying before was, "I want to leave my husband, but I'd like him to at least have his parents when I do."

Denise: No, I feel if I did leave him, because he keeps saying he wants to leave in a year, it would be easier if he didn't have anyone else. But I feel so sad that he has nobody. And not even friends, like women have friends. He doesn't have male friends to play tennis with. And he's so unhappy and angry. I want to give him some of what I'm getting from meditating and yoga and everything.

And you would want to do this in the year prior to your leaving.

Denise: In fact, I would want him not to be angry and unhappy. I want him to want me. It would be nice if he didn't want me to leave.

If he didn't want you to leave, you wouldn't go?

Denise: I can't be alone.

But is that a different statement from "I want to be with him?"

Denise: Right now I don't want to be with him.

Now, if you made him happy in the way you're describing to me, would you then leave him when you've got him to the happy point?

Denise: No.

So if he were happy, you would stay with him. What you're saying is that the reason you're not going to stay with him, or in some sense are thinking about leaving, is because of his unhappiness.

Denise: Yes, I don't think I should take even another year of his abuse. My daughter's a senior and I think until she goes to college I will have to stick it out.

Right, the fear then is of being alone, spending a lot of time alone.

Denise: I've never been alone and it's sort of an exciting thought. If he left my house, I would be thrilled, but he wants me to leave. I don't want to lose my home.

So are you excited about being alone?

Denise: Yes, I am excited, and that sort of scares me also.

You're excited about being alone, but before this you said, "I just simply can't be alone."

Denise: I'm excited about being alone because I would probably go out and find somebody else to replace him.

So your excitement is the possibility of someone replacing him, not being alone?

Denise: Yes.

Okay, because you said a minute ago, "I'm excited about being alone," but now we have a sub-clause which says, "I'm excited about being alone because I'll find someone to replace the person I don't want to be with."

Denise: Although I know I should be alone.

Okay, this sounds like a conflict.

Denise: Yes.

In other words, these are the levels of the mental experience you are having. Number one, "My husband is very unhappy and he abuses me, and because of that I want to leave." That's number one. I'm just sort of outlining it, yes?

Denise: I want him to leave. He wants me to leave.

Number two, it looks to you like you're going to be the one who actually has to leave because he wants the house, right?

Denise: Right.

Okay, that's number two. And you don't want to leave the house.

Denise: Right.

A sub-clause after that is, "If I could stay in the house and he could leave, then part of this conflict is over."

Denise: Right.

Okay, then number three is, "I am excited about living alone."

Denise: Yes.

Number four is, "I am afraid about living alone."

Denise: Right.

Number five is, "I'm afraid about how excited I am about living alone."

Denise: Yes.

Number six is, "I am excited about living alone because I'm going to find someone to replace this man I don't like."

Denise: I do like him.

Oh, then he doesn't like you. Is that right?

Denise: Right.

Okay, I mean, "If only he liked me, then I wouldn't leave," is an obvious statement, yes?

Denise: Right, so how can I go home and make things better?

Why do you have to go home to make things better? Where is the conflict taking place? Just so we understand each other as we speak. Who is having this conflict right now?

Denise: I am. He's playing tennis, probably.

I'm not saying that he's not having his own conflict, but the conflict that you just described is your own.

Denise: Right.

Now this is an interesting question, and I'm not sure it can be easily answered. This is not a right/wrong question. How much of your conflict would still exist if the circumstances changed, and how much of it sits inside you no matter what?
If he started liking you, would your conflicts go away?

Denise: No, it still would be there — unless he became spiritual, unless he became somebody else.

Okay, so what you're saying is that it is not only that he doesn't like you, but that he's not spiritual.

Denise: He's angry, and controlling and very unhappy. I lived with these things for years, and now they are incredibly big and annoying because I see them.

But you like him.

Denise: Eighty percent of the time.

Okay, so all this hardship with him is about twenty percent of the time.

Denise: No, every three weeks he becomes a monster for a day.

Right.

Denise: Actually, the last year and a half.

He's been a monster.

Denise: When he became fifty, he said, "I want you out. I'm happier when you're gone. I want to get a divorce." And he got very depressed.

Now, if he didn't change in any other way, but he said, "I like you very much and I want you here," would that be enough?

Denise: It would have been enough.

But?

Denise: Five months ago.

But what has the five months brought that doesn't make it enough?

Denise: Now he would have to do other things that I would want him to do.

Such as?

Denise: Read the books I buy, do yoga, communicate with me, which is something that he never did.

So it is more than just him liking you. You want a different kind of person, someone who's willing to communicate with you, to share your fundamental beliefs.

Denise: I want to be with somebody I'm comfortable with and not afraid of. And I'm afraid when I'm with him. Even when he's nice, I'm on my guard.

Because he so easily becomes a monster?

Denise: No, because I'm just always afraid of him.

What are you afraid of? Can you tell, or is it too hard?

Denise: His little criticisms, you know, that are constant, even when he's nice. I'm afraid that he's going to embarrass me in front of a friend.

He puts you down in front of other people?

Denise: No, he says what he wants to the friend and then makes them feel bad.

I'm not sure I understand that.

Denise: He will say something to a girlfriend of mine. I've lost a lot of friends because of him.

What kind of things would he say?

Denise: Ummm, with one girl he carried in the groceries or something, and she said, "Oh, my father always carried in the groceries and put them away for my mother." And he said, "Oh, that's why your father's dead." And this girl almost cried. Things like that.

He would say something that is so inappropriate that it drove your friends away.

Denise: Yes, and yet he's still also very charming, and very nice, and very responsible and a very good person. I really don't know if I should tell him that he has to call his parents.

How would that solve your conflict?

Denise: I can't imagine my mother just calling and saying, "I'm not happy with this relationship. That's it. Goodbye." I'd be over at her house immediately, like she's sick or something.

I'm not sure I follow that. I wonder if you could....

Denise: It's strange when your parents decide not to see you ever again.

Oh, yes, it is. I see what you're saying.

Denise: And for him not to pursue it.... I would pursue it if it was my mother.

Well, if you told him to call his parents, would he do it?

Denise: No, he would be too afraid. He used to call them every Sunday as a duty call.

Does he really want a relationship with them?

Denise: He feels he's not good enough to have one.

Good enough for them?

Denise: Yeah.

It's not that he doesn't like them or anything. It's that he doesn't feel good enough for them.

Denise: But they made him feel he's not good enough, because his father's a doctor and he only became a teacher. And now they're making all of us feel that we're not good enough.

The duty call was simply a way to please them?

Denise: Yeah.

But now they've stopped calling him.

Denise: They never called us.

You mean they never called at all?

Denise: Right.

So this isn't anything new, is it?

Denise: No.

You're saying that the relationship never existed, except that he called them.

Denise: It existed three times a year when we would meet them for dinner.

Why does it surprise you that he doesn't reach out to them, since they haven't responded to him for so long?

Denise: I don't think you can disown your children for no reason.

But he's been disowned for quite some time, hasn't he?

Denise: He feels this is because he was adopted as a teenager, but I don't think that's true.

But didn't you say to me before that they never called him anyway, that they just waited for his call?

Denise: He felt it a duty to call them every week.

But they didn't call him?

Denise: They called maybe once a year when they came home from Europe, just to say they were home.

But you're also saying that they suddenly cut him off.

Denise: Yes, and my daughter.

This is where I'm a bit confused. I'm wondering if you could help me out. Did he ever have a relationship with them since you've been married?

Denise: We saw them three times a year for dinner.

In your estimation, is that a relationship?

Denise: Not a good one, no.

On the other side of this, you are saying to me that they suddenly cut off the relationship.

Denise: Yes.

Well, what relationship did they suddenly cut off?

Denise: Seeing us three times a year for dinner, coming over to our house.

A year has gone by and those three times came and went.

Denise: We haven't seen them since Christmas.

Okay, so the little bit of relationship that existed is over in your estimation.

Denise: My mother-in-law said she was tired of making believe there was a happy family.

Okay, and do you agree with her that there was a make-believe going on?

Denise: Oh, definitely.

What do you suggest that she does? I mean where does that go? I'm trying to settle into what you're saying because there are so many things involved in this. On the one hand, you're saying there wasn't really a relationship except three times a year and one phone call a year. And now you're saying that that little bit of relationship suddenly got cut off. And then you're saying that you were upset because she said they're tired of pretending to be a happy family. That bothered you. Then I asked you whether it's true that you've been pretending to be a happy family and you said, "Yes."

What I hear you saying distinctly, Denise, and I just want to be sure I understand, is that there has been no real relationship and no happiness since you've known them.

Denise: The times we were together were very pleasant.

"Were very pleasant." I thought you said it was something like a handshake.

Denise: They were pleasant but, you know, a different kind of communication.

Right.

Denise: We don't know what's really going on with them, and they don't know what's really going on with us.

It was formal. It was on the surface.

Denise: Very much, yes. But that's how they are. They are very formal. It's still strange to just cut off your family. They have no other family, and they're old.

I mean when he was fifteen or sixteen were they warm and loving to him?

Denise: They adopted him when he was fourteen.

Well, when he was fifteen, sixteen, seventeen, were they warm and loving to him?

Denise: They expected a little baby. They got a fourteen-year-old boy. They gave him everything materially.

But?

Denise: No warmth.

Right, and also you said they belittled him because his father's a doctor and he became a teacher.

Denise: They keep saying that so-and-so's son is a brain surgeon, and so-and-so's son is a scientist. They constantly do that. They still do that.

These are fairly rough people to hang out with. I mean, that's my impression.

Denise: Yes, that's why my husband is like he is.

And that's why he doesn't want to talk with them, don't you think? I mean maybe that's part of it.

Denise: Well he's so hurt. He is very hurt.

Yeah, and they hurt him fairly consistently. He feels he's disappointed them fundamentally. That's very difficult.

Denise: And now he doesn't want me, which is strange because he lost his parents during the war. He lost the people who took him in their house after the war. He lost his first wife.

How did he lose his first wife, through divorce?

Denise: Yes, she was in a mental hospital before they were married and after.

They were married before she went into the hospital?

Denise: She was in the hospital before he married her and he never knew it, and she was sick while they were married.

I see. And then she had a breakdown again?

Denise: After they were separated, yeah. He ran away from the situation.

And now he wants to....?

Denise: And now he wants to throw me out, which is to have no caretakers.

You would call yourself a caretaker to him? That's the way you would identify yourself or characterize yourself?

Denise: Yes, I think he's trying to get rid of the last person....

No, no. I'm asking if you are a caretaker to him? Is that the way you see yourself?

Denise: No, no.

So you're not a caretaker?

Denise: No.

So when you say to me that he's throwing out the last caretaker, maybe the last caretaker is already gone. I mean, if you're not a caretaker to him, then how is he throwing out his last caretaker?

Denise: Well, it depends on what you mean by caretaker.

That's what I'm asking.

Denise: I cook and clean. I iron his shirts. I could be caring much more. I could be giving....

You're saying that you take care of him technically. The technical things you take care of. But what is the other caretaker that you're speaking of?

Denise: The one who can be honest and talk and share and be a friend.

And you can't do that because he's not willing?

Denise: I've always been afraid, yes.

Wait, say that again.

Denise: I've always been afraid to talk to him even when I could be honest.

In other words you're saying that this "always been afraid" includes courtship, early marriage, right through?

Denise: Yeah.

So you're saying to me that part of the reason you can't communicate with him is because you're afraid to.

Denise: Yeah.

Okay, and you have been afraid since you've known him.

Denise: Yeah.

Is that fear based on something he did or said?

Denise: I think at the beginning you're on your best behavior and put on an act.

You did that.

Denise: I guess I didn't know any better then.

Sure, so you're saying that the reason you didn't communicate in the beginning was because you were putting on an act.

Denise: Yes.

And then later on, as the years progressed?

Denise: I could never tell him how I felt about anything.

How do you know that?

Denise: Because big things happened and I couldn't tell him how I felt.

But let's take the word "couldn't." When you tried he stopped you?

Denise: No.

Then how do you know you couldn't?

Denise: I assumed how he felt.

And on what basis did you make this assumption?

Denise: On his actions.

Okay, and what were his actions that created the assumption that you couldn't tell him how you felt?

Denise: He was very controlling and strong.

And by "controlling," what exactly do you mean? Just so I'm following how you got to the assumption that you couldn't tell him how you felt. How does that relate to controlling?

Denise: I had to do everything he said.

And what was the threat if you didn't?

Denise: He would leave or throw me out.

Did he say that, early on?

Denise: Yes.

So this thing about him wanting to throw you out is not new? It's been consistent right along?

Denise: Yes.

It isn't really the last six months or a year that you're talking about. You're talking about your whole married life.

Denise: No, no, just the last six months or a year. But he has used this before.

It's not been as harsh as it is now, but he's used it before.

Denise: He used it before seriously on several occasions.

And you said, "I'm hurt, I'm angry, I'm upset," something like that, and he would say, "If you keep talking like that I want you out of here."

Denise: No, it was....no, it was, I think, important things.

Well, an important thing being what?

Denise: I had a baby with Down's Syndrome. I was living with Allan a year. I lived with him for four years.

Allan is your husband.

Denise: Yes.

And this was prior to your being married.

Denise: Yeah.

Was this his child?

Denise: Yes.

Okay, go ahead.

Denise: He told me I couldn't keep the baby.

And did you want to?

Denise: Yes.

You wanted to because....? I just want to understand. You wanted to because you felt a real love for the baby. Is that right?

Denise: More than anything. I thought that it was a special gift from God.

Beautiful....and he said what?

Denise: He said that if we don't find a home for him, he's going to leave. And every day he went to work, I took the baby home, and for two months, every day, he had a list of places I had to call.

A list of places you had to call.

Denise: Yes.

He wouldn't call them.

Denise: No.

And the reason that you complied with this was because you would rather give up the baby than be alone.

Denise: Yes, I finally....we did find a home, and when I found out that the state wasn't going to pay, I ran away with my eight-year-old son.

Oh, there was a son....

Denise: From my first marriage.

And what about the baby?

Denise: I left him with my husband and he called the social worker who came and took the baby to the hospital.

Now this running away with your eight-year-old son, do you remember the motivation, the context, in which it was taking place?

Denise: It was to save Allan from paying $125 a week.

To this home?

Denise: To the foster mother.

For who, for the Down's Syndrome baby?

Denise: Yeah.

Oh, you mean that if he didn't have a wife the state would pay?

Denise: I knew the baby would get into the home.

You said to me a minute ago — now, I'm trying to follow you — the reason you ran away with your eight-year-old son was to save Allan $125 a week in fees to the home.

Denise: In fees to the state, to the foster home. The foster home was found.

How does the act of running away accomplish that savings?

Denise: Because I left a letter and he called the social worker and they took the baby.

Because the baby didn't have a mother, the state was willing to....

Denise: He just called and said, "My wife left, and now I have a month-old baby and I can't take care of it."

Let's go back to that, Denise. How long did you stay away with your eight-year-old son?

Denise: About five days.

Where did you go?

Denise: To Brooklyn, to my girlfriend's house. He knew where I was.

How did you feel at that time about leaving the baby behind?

Denise: Partly numb.

You don't remember feelings?

Denise: I think I was just blocking everything.

And did you see the baby after that?

Denise: Yes, every two months or so until he was two.

And then?

Denise: I got pregnant immediately. I had a baby ten months after him. If I didn't get pregnant, I don't know what would have happened. I may have taken him back. I should have taken him back when he was two.

This "should" on the basis of the way you felt about the baby?

Denise: Yes, he was a beautiful little boy. I have pictures of him in the playpen with my daughter and my older son.

You really loved him.

Denise: And when he was two, this woman could adopt the baby. I felt the love and warmth in her home.

Who was this now?

Denise: The woman who adopted him.

Okay, she was willing to adopt a Down's Syndrome baby.

Denise: She had a nine-year-old son who had Down's Syndrome and was deaf and epileptic, and a sixteen-year-old daughter.

Right.

Denise: And they were very beautiful and religious people. And I asked her if she would consider adopting him because the state was considering taking us to court at that time.

For what? What were they taking you to court for?

Denise: They took us to court twice. The first time I said Allan isn't the father and I got away with it.

Why did you do that?

Denise: To save him from paying money. I said I was away at camp during the summer and I got pregnant and I don't know who the father was.

Did he know that was what you were doing?

Denise: I thought of that and we talked it over and he said that it was a good idea.

And this was how much money?

Denise: They wanted $125 a week.

They took you to court because they disbelieved your story all of a sudden.

Denise: Oh, yes, six or seven months later we got court papers. Some lawyer said that they couldn't get away with it. They were going to order blood tests. And I asked the woman if she would adopt him, and she said, "I thought you were just going to take him away." She said that she really wanted to adopt him.
    Then they didn't take me to court. I just had to go and sign the papers to give him up for adoption, and it was rough.

What is your memory about your feelings when you went to visit the baby in the hospital?

Denise: I didn't visit him in the hospital.

Oh, I'm sorry. When you went to visit him when he was in the custody of someone else, what were your feelings when you saw your son?

Denise: Terrific love.

You felt a real strong love.

Denise: Yes, I wanted him so badly, and I think that's what I was referring to in Brownsville. How do you forget someone? I think I've always hated Allan for this, and I don't know how I can ever forgive him.

I can really understand that. Now I want to tell you what I heard so that we're on common ground. You had a Down's Syndrome baby and you loved this baby a lot, yes?

Denise: Yes.

And Allan said to you, "We must get rid of this baby. We must throw out our child," yes? "Otherwise if you don't, I'm going to leave you."

Denise: And when I got pregnant again, I had to go through the amniocentesis.

To make sure it wouldn't happen again.

Denise: And they don't tell you this, but they called me six weeks later and they said no cells grew. And I didn't think anything like that could happen and they said you can come in and have it done again. I wouldn't find out until I was five months pregnant, and I would never have an abortion if I were five months pregnant. I don't even know if I would have an abortion in two months. I thought I would just run away. And he told me if I don't have the test and there's anything wrong with the baby, I'm not coming home from the hospital.

You mean you wouldn't be allowed in the house?

Denise: That if there was anything wrong with the second baby, I could never come home.

Right.

Denise: That's what I meant when I said he threatened to throw me out.

Did you go for the next amniocentesis?

Denise: No.

And the next baby, was it a boy or a girl?

Denise: It was a girl, Louise. She's seventeen now.

And what is your remembrance of what you felt about Louise when she was born, or during those early years? Was it the same quality of love you were feeling toward....?

Denise: Oh yes, tremendous.

Did you name this child with Down's Syndrome?

Denise: We were going to name him after Allan's father and my grandfather.

And then at the point he said to you, "You must get rid of this baby," you became frightened of his leaving, of Allan's leaving.

Denise: He didn't even tell me he was divorced.

He had never told you that he had been married before.

Denise: I knew that he was married, but he got a divorce in Mexico the summer before I moved in with him. But he didn't tell me he got a divorce. He didn't tell me he was divorced until after Louise was born.

I realize now that I didn't hear something that you said which was, that at the point you had this baby, you weren't married.

Denise: I wasn't married when I had my daughter either, and for two years I wasn't married until I threatened to leave with his daughter unless we got married, and then he said, okay.

You threatened to leave with her unless you got married. He responded to that threat.

Denise: Yeah, I forced him into getting married.

Much the same way he forced you — just so we understand this — much the same way he forced you to have your son Mark taken to another place to live, right? I mean it's the same basic strategy. And he responded in the way you did. He actually submitted. He didn't want you to leave with his daughter.

Denise: I gave up my child for him because I saw him getting very loving with the baby.

Louise?

Denise: No, with Mark.

Oh, with Mark.

Denise: I mean he was like six weeks old and I saw if we had him another two weeks that there was no way he would be able to let him go and then Allan would hate me forever.

He was falling in love with the baby.

Denise: I saw that.

You felt that if you didn't act quickly, Allan would hate you forever.

Denise: Yes, our relationship was not good. It was not a good home.

So you thought it was better to have Mark taken somewhere else because the home life wasn't good.

Denise: Yes.

Are you saying to me, just so I understand....

Denise: I didn't feel he was in a good home then. Years later I realized that he was much better off with good people and loving people in a good home.

So it was partly your decision to take Mark to another home. It wasn't just under Allan's threat.

Denise: It was under the threat.

But you just said, part of the reason....

Denise: I got so scared when I saw the way he held him....

That he loved him.

Denise: Yes, and I got so scared.

Now, your fear of Allan loving Mark consisted of the idea that if Allan loved Mark, he couldn't give Mark up, and you had to give Mark up because Allan didn't love Mark. I'm struggling right in there.

Denise: He didn't want him because God did this to him.

God was punishing Allan for Mark via the Down's Syndrome.

Denise: Yes.

And the way Allan decided to deal with the punishment was to remove the child from his life.

Denise: Yeah.

But you also were feeling, at this time, that this wasn't a good home for the child — this child that you felt was a gift from God.

Denise: Not at that time. Years later....

Oh, at that time you didn't feel that way.

Denise: At that time I just wanted him.

You wanted him. Now I understand. It was years later that you thought back and said, "We did the right thing."

Denise: Right.

I just want to understand what you said about Allan loving Mark. If Allan loved Mark, would Allan still have insisted on having Mark leave?

Denise: Yes.

And you didn't want that to happen because you felt there would be a huge resentment from Allan toward you.

Denise: I couldn't have him on a waiting list and keep him two years and then have him leave for a school or a hospital. Everything was a two-year waiting list.

But how would Allan's love for Mark affect whether the child would be on a waiting list or not?

Denise: He would never consent to keep him. It would hurt to let him go, but he would never keep him.

But his love would prolong Marks's stay in the house. So at that point you acted. You acted more swiftly than you thought Allan would. So there was an element of decision in this.

Denise: Yes.

In other words, Allan wanted the child to go for one reason. But Allan was also beginning to feel a great deal of love for this child, and you were afraid that if Allan felt too much love it would prolong Mark's stay. Mark would then end up on a waiting list for two years and that would be a genuine problem.

Denise: He was on a two-year waiting list when he came into this woman's home.

So you acted swiftly at that time.

Denise: Yes.

And the way you acted swiftly was what?

Denise: I wrote the letter and took my other son and left.

That was a way not only to save Allan money, but also to get Mark in a good home.

Denise: Yes.

Initially you said that the reason you ran away was to save Allan $125, but there's a little more to it than that, right? You also wanted to make sure that Mark got to a home quickly so that he didn't have to wait two years.

Denise: Yes.

So you accomplished two different things by running away. You saved Allan money, but the reason you acted so quickly wasn't just to save Allan money. It was also a way to deal with a desire of your own.

Denise: In my pain, I couldn't keep him another week or two and then let him go.

So there were three reasons for running away. One was to save Allan money, and we'll put that at the bottom of the list right now. The other was to make sure that Mark got into a home that was good. And the third was because your pain was getting so great that you perceived no other choice. That's totally understandable. Your pain was mounting. You had a gift from God to take care of and you felt that you had to give this gift from God up. Otherwise Allan would leave you.

Denise: And Allan's parents, they just said, he just said, "Do you want to see my son?" And they just said, "How much money do you need?" That's what they said, and they never mentioned him.

"How much money do you need?" means, "How much money do you need to get rid of him?"

Denise: Yes.

I feel that, Denise. I feel that. That's a tough kernel down in there. You know what I'm saying? I understand. I really understand.

Denise: And every year on his birthday, it's like I know his birthday is coming. It's the day after my other son's birthday, and all that day I'm very sad. I usually cry that night. Allan never even knows his birthday. And when it's my daughter's birthday, I say to myself, "Now you have two seventeen-year-olds." And then his birthday comes, and he's eighteen. So I have a seventeen-year-old and an eighteen-year-old. And Allan doesn't even know. He never mentions him at all.

He never mentions Mark.

Denise: He mentioned him a few months ago. We were jogging and walking on the track.

And what did he say?

Denise: He said, "How can you believe in God?"

Because?

Denise: "Because he gave you a retarded child."

And what did you say?

Denise: I said that that's karma, and being that he's not with me, I'm going to have to have him in another life.

And what did Allan say?

Denise: Nothing, he thinks I'm crazy.

This thought of having him in another life is almost like a dream, isn't it? I mean it's almost something you would want. You love this child. It's something you would actually like to experience, isn't that right?

Denise: My daughter now wants a job working with retarded children this winter.

Have you told her about Mark?

165

Denise: She saw the pictures of her and him together. I told her about him when she was nine. Allan said, "What did you do that for?"

He said that to you?

Denise: Allan said that. I told him weeks later that I told her.

And he was upset with you.

Denise: Yes.

Did you feel that he was angry?

Denise: Yes. He said, "Now she's going to think she can never have normal children."

That was his concern, that she could never have normal children?

Denise: I think now she's thinking that she would probably like to meet him. He lives very close.

When was the last time you saw Mark?

Denise: When he was two.

And he's now seventeen, eighteen?

Denise: Eighteen. I've heard about him through a friend.

And I guess it's because of a sensitivity to the situation that you haven't gone to see him. You don't want to interfere.

Denise: I'd like to sit across the street and look at him.

Have you done that?

Denise: No, I'm afraid. I know if I called she would let me see him any time.

She would.

Denise: I just can't.

What are you afraid of?

Denise: I feel guilty.

You're afraid of your guilt when you see Mark?

Denise: I told him I'd never give him away.

You said that to him or you thought that to him?

Denise: I said that to him when he was two days old.

You knew he had Down's Syndrome then and you said, "I love you so much that I will never give you away."

Denise: Right.

And then you did.

Denise: I don't know; maybe he'd hate me; I don't know.

But there's a desire to sit across the street and see him outside. And you're afraid because you feel terribly guilty or you're afraid because you feel so much longing and love?

Denise: It's a panic.

It's a panic attack. Now when you ran away and left for five days, and I said to you, "How did you feel?" you said, "Probably numb, I probably shut it all down." Do you suspect that the panic you're feeling in relation to Mark, about seeing him,

167

is a similar kind of shutdown that you experienced for those five days when you didn't know what you were feeling?

Denise: Yeah, I blocked it all. I know I was at this friend's house. I remember calling Allan a few times.

Yes, but you must have been scared, weren't you? Scared of the guilt, scared of the love, scared of the situation?

Denise: Yes, very much.

There was panic, and there's panic still.

Denise: Yes.

In other words, what isn't resolved at this moment is the panic in relationship to an experience that occurred eighteen years ago which was very, very painful. There's still a panic in relationship to this experience which hasn't been resolved.

Denise: Yeah.

Not all of the panic relates to Mark. Some of it relates to Allan, doesn't it, your feelings toward him concerning what happened?

Denise: Yes.

What I hear you saying is, "I don't know if I can forgive this man."

Denise: I don't feel like I could ever forgive him unless he changed so much and became loving and kind, if he became so different. He's so angry and so unhappy.

And you?

Denise: I'm not angry, and I'm not unhappy.

You're not angry?

Denise: No.

What do you have to forgive then, if you're not angry?

Denise: (Silence) Then I am angry.

Yes, don't you think so?

Denise: Yes.

It's a tough story you just told me, Denise. It's a very tough story you just told me. Don't you think that maybe....

Denise: That's why I want to make things better for him.

For Allan?

Denise: I feel that I did something bad to him.

You did something bad to Allan?

Denise: Yes, that's why I want to give him his parents back, or give him my family.

Listen, listen now. You did something bad to Allan. You would like to give him his real parents back, yes?

Denise: Yes, I moved in with him.

You do hear that, that you did something bad to Allan and you would like to give Allan his parents back.

Denise: Yes.

Okay, can you feel me, Denise? I love you very much. I hope you know that. I'm really with you here. I feel for you. I feel my own heart bursting open with understanding and appreciation for your life. I understand you've been through something extremely difficult. I want to follow you down this road. Are you angry at Allan?

Denise: Yes.

Because he forced you to give a child away that you loved. He did that by threatening to abandon you.

Denise: Yes.

And then you said to me, "The reason I want to give him his parents back is because I did something wrong." What is the "something wrong" that you did, to your husband, Allan?

Denise: He didn't want any children, and I moved in and I got pregnant immediately.

And that was just your end of it. It was your lack of responsibility that ended up making you pregnant. You were the responsible party in getting pregnant.

Denise: I didn't get pregnant by myself.

No, you didn't. So it wasn't just you that was the responsible party. You mutually joined, had a sexual experience which was risky and you got pregnant. So how does that become something that you did bad?

Denise: Because I wanted him to marry me.

Did you make him believe that you were not going to get pregnant?

Denise: I think so.

Do you think so or do you sort of know so?

Denise: I don't remember.

But you think you sort of led him to believe that in some way you were protected, or were at a time in your cycle when you weren't going to get pregnant?

Denise: I don't think we were careful, that's all. I think it's both our faults. Because I had a daughter ten months later which is impossible.

So it wasn't that you tricked him?

Denise: I went to the doctor because my stomach was getting bigger, and I thought I had a tumor. And he said, "You're pregnant," and I said, "I can't be pregnant. I just had a baby."

So both of you chose to have sex and you ended up pregnant. Then you had a child with Down's Syndrome and you loved this child. And the question which comes to me is, how did you do something bad to Allan?

Denise: He told me I got pregnant.

He told you that.

Denise: Yes.

But Denise, is that true? He told you you got pregnant by yourself?

Denise: He blamed me.

And on what basis did he blame you? What did he say? On what evidence did he blame you?

Denise: Just because he didn't want to have any children. He didn't want to get married.

He didn't want to get married. He didn't want to have children, but he had sex with you and you got pregnant. And he knew that sex leads to pregnancy sometimes.

Denise: But it didn't before I moved in. I didn't get pregnant before I moved in. It was a whole year. I saw him on weekends, so I guess we felt I wasn't going to get pregnant.

You didn't pretend that you were taking birth control pills or something like that, did you?

Denise: No.

So you both knew, on some level, that there was a risk in having sex.

Denise: Right.

And you believe to this day, Denise — I just want to understand this — that getting pregnant was something you did to Allan?

Denise: Yes, because I moved in. Because I threatened him. I said if you don't let me move in, then I'm going to see other people. I can't be coming here every weekend with a six-year-old kid. It's not right.

So you made the threat again, "I will abandon you if you don't do what I want."

Denise: Yes. He said, "You can move in, but don't ever ask for anything else."

Now the thing that you did bad to Allan was to say, "This isn't good for my six-year-old son to be visiting a man only on the weekends." You didn't break in, right? He said okay. He agreed, even though there was a threat, so how is it that you did something bad?

Denise: I guess I did something bad because the baby wasn't perfect.

Just so we understand this, a woman conceived a child with a man. And the child is born with Down's Syndrome. The woman loves the child and the man disapproves. And you are saying that it is a bad thing on the part of the woman to have had a child like that. That's what you're saying, because it's her responsibility to have a perfect baby to please the man.

Denise: That's how he made me feel.

But as you look at it now, does it concern you a little bit that you subscribed to such an idea?

Denise: That's how I felt. I don't really believe it that much.

Even though you felt this baby was a gift from God, you assumed that you did something bad to Allan because you didn't have a perfect baby.

Denise: He tried to make me feel that.

By belittling you, belittling the baby, or no? How did he try to make you feel that?

Denise: By trying to find a place to put him.

By bringing home the list of names of places to put the child. That's how he made you believe that you had done a bad thing?

Denise: Yes, by not wanting to take him home from the hospital.

This mother love you felt toward Mark, did it have anything to do with whether the baby was perfect or not?

Denise: No.

It was a perfect baby, wasn't it?

Denise: The most beautiful baby I ever had.

So what you're really saying to me is not, "I gave Allan an imperfect baby." You're saying, "I disappointed Allan," right?

Denise: Right.

You're saying that even though this was the most perfect baby you ever had, Allan disapproved and therefore you did something bad. That's a slightly different statement, is it not, from saying you gave Allan an imperfect baby?

Denise: It's the right way to say it.

It is. You had a perfect baby that you loved very much, and Allan was upset. Therefore you thought you had done something bad.

Denise: I feel less angry toward him.

Well, when did you feel more angry towards him?

Denise: A few minutes ago.

You did. You felt it running through your body. It lasted about how long?

Denise: It was there.

Why do you now feel less angry with Allan? Just so I understand.

Denise: I think I feel less guilty.

That's very interesting and very useful. In other words, you're saying that the anger at Allan was somehow a reaction to your own guilt.

Denise: Yes.

And now that you feel less guilty, you also feel less angry.

Denise: Yes.

There's something you said a while back that was very beautiful, about wanting to give Allan his parents back because you had done something bad. Do you think you were speaking about Allan?

Denise: I don't understand.

Is it really Allan who you would like to give parents back to?

Denise: I can't get Mark back.

You can't, I know, just like you can't give Allan his parents back, yes?

Denise: Right.

But wouldn't you like to give Mark his parents back?

Denise: I'd like to give him his sister.

But wouldn't you also like to sit across the street and see Mark?

Denise: Yes.

And isn't that because you're his mother and you love him?

Denise: Yes.

And on that basis, part of you would like to have him back, have his parents back?

Denise: Yes.

That's very beautiful, Denise. It's absolutely right. I mean, is it that you feel you did something bad to Allan or do you feel that you did something bad to Mark?

Denise: To Mark. Allan did something bad to me and to himself and to his daughter.

That's a different story, isn't it?

Denise: Yeah.

That's a different story. There's a part of you that feels you would love to give Mark his parents back, and maybe in that sense, you feel something bad was done. There's another part of you that understands that he ended up in a very fine place and that you were not irresponsible, isn't that right?

Denise: Yes, they live in a beautiful home. His mother was mother of the year five years ago.

That's beautiful.

Denise: And when I read about her in the paper, it was very horrible to me.

I'll bet it was.

Denise: Especially when the reporter said that the mother didn't want the child and this woman was the first person to adopt a retarded child in Crawfield County, and that she took him and named him Mark. I named him after my grandfather.

And his mother did want him, isn't that right? His mother did want him. The newspaper didn't report the truth.

Denise: And I cut it out and I have the article hidden away somewhere. I never showed it to Allan. I can't communicate to him.

I understand.

Denise: I couldn't even show him this article.

You were abused, don't you think so?

Denise: Yes.

In a very basic way, you were abused, at least from what I'm hearing. A man forced his wife to give up her beloved child to satisfy his image of what a child should be, and she did. It has hurt her ever since, and she has never been able to be honest with her husband since.

Denise: I'd feel like he'd leave if I was honest.

Now Denise, without attaching any morality to this, isn't there a part of you that would like to force him to feel something like what you felt?

Denise: I tried.

You did. How did you try?

Denise: Ten years ago, we went to Marriage Encounter and it was beautiful. And after that we joined a group and we met with some other couples once a month. Each month one couple would present. And the month we were going to present, I wrote the whole presentation on the story of Mark, and we presented it to these other couples.

"We" did, or you did?

Denise: Allan and I.

Did he know that's what you were going to do?

Denise: He wrote his part also. It contained a lot of anger and pain about what God had done to him.

Like giving him an imperfect child.

Denise: Yes.

Okay.

Denise: And we presented it. And the couples, they wrote us beautiful letters. But he had a hard time even getting to the point to do it. He didn't want to and then he finally did. And after it was over, he never talked about it again.

And how was that trying to get him to feel....oh, by sharing your feelings.

Denise: I wrote everything down, and he wrote his, and we dialogued together.

And did you tell it then the way you told it to me?

Denise: More or less.

So you told it the way he didn't want to hear it.

Denise: Yes, and he told it the way I didn't want to hear it, and we were together in a dialogue.

Are there other ways you tried to get him to hear it?

Denise: That's the only time we ever talked about it.

No, I mean more indirectly than that. Are there other ways in which you wanted him to feel what you felt?

Denise: No, no.

No? You've always been very caring with him, wanting to make sure he feels good.

Denise: Yes.

So you pretty much held it in.

Denise: Yes, I just held it in. I still hold it in.

What is the "it" that you're holding in?

Denise: I have this frustration.

What is the frustration?

Denise: That I can't do anything about anything.

That's what you're holding in?

Denise: Oh, I'm probably holding in a lot of anger.

When you say "probably," it's because you're not sure.

Denise: I don't feel angry.

When we were together last you said, if I understood you correctly, "I've been feeling numb for as long as I can remember, and this is the first time I've been feeling something." It was painful, but there was hope in it, right?

Denise: Yes.

You've been feeling numb since then.

Denise: I was never allowed to have feelings.

Or you never allowed yourself to have feelings, either one.

Denise: My family didn't have feelings. Allan never allowed feelings.

So you've been numb for your....

Denise: My children don't have feelings; my whole house, nobody has feelings. And Allan was angry if you had feelings.

And it bothers you every time Allan gets angry? I mean, does Allan's anger create anxiety in you?

Denise: Yes.

Whenever he gets angry, you get panicky?

Denise: I just learned to leave the room.

Leave the room because? Earlier, you had said that the reason you had to leave Allan was because he was angry all the time, isn't that right? Or angry a lot?

Denise: He's angry a lot, but he's also unhappy.

When he gets angry, you get scared, don't you?

Denise: When he yells, I'm scared. I'm always afraid of him.

You're always afraid of him because he's angry a lot?

Denise: He's angry a lot.

He's angry a lot and you're afraid of him.

Denise: Yes, and when he's not angry, I can't communicate. If I say anything, he gets angry.

Okay, and when he gets angry, you get afraid.

Denise: He corners me.

He corners you physically?

Denise: Yes, I think he's going to hit me. I pull my glasses off immediately if I have them on.

Has he ever hit you?

Denise: Yes.

In the face?

Denise: He punched me in the head a couple of times.

Because you did what?

Denise: Because I told him he should hire someone to fix the fence instead of doing it himself. And then he thought that he couldn't do a good job, so he just came over and started cornering me and punching me — not hard. And then I ran down into the basement and he locked me in. I thought of calling the police.

You thought of it, but you didn't.

Denise: No, but I should if this happens again. I told him I thought of it.

Right.

Denise: This is just a few months ago.

So you're saying that Allan is violent and you're afraid of his violence. You want to leave, but you're afraid to leave. Isn't that part of it, because you're afraid of being left alone?

Denise: Yes, and my daughter doesn't want me to leave.

Yes, I understand that. That's another factor. One way of describing your relationship to Allan is that it is either abusive or potentially abusive. He's hit you; he's locked you in the basement; you thought of calling the police; he made you give your child up; and there's more I'm sure.

Denise: Yeah.

There's a history of fearfulness in relation to this man.

Denise: Yes.

And yet there's also a sense somehow that it is better to be with him than it is to be alone. The loneliness is more dangerous — is that right, Denise — than the violence?

Denise: I'm dependent. I've never been alone.

Yes, and it's better to have this man who hurts you than to be hurt by aloneness.

Denise: I don't know what the loneliness is. It would probably feel good.

Denise, you don't know what loneliness is?

Denise: No, I don't.

Do you think that the life you've been describing to me is a life that isn't about loneliness?

Denise: It is, but I call a lot of people.

You have friends, but you would have those friends anyway, wouldn't you?

Denise: I don't know.

They'd leave you if you left Allan.

Denise: No, more would come around.

Sure, because Allan, you were saying before, would drive your friends away. Where is the lack of aloneness with Allan?

Denise: It's part of my family.

I'm not sure I understand that. He destructed your family. Didn't he send your child away?

Denise: And he sent my twenty-six-year-old son away. He left when he was eighteen to join the service.

Because Allan was so rough on him. He belittled him.

Denise: Yes.

Allan told him he wasn't worth much. Why are you afraid to leave Allan?

Denise: I want him to leave me, I think.

It would be easier if he left you.

Denise: I want my house.

Yes, I understand.

Denise: I want my daughter.

That's perfectly understandable. If you left Allan, he would take your daughter.

Denise: She would stay with him. They're very close.

She said that?

Denise: No, she's in the high school.

Is he rough on her?

Denise: No.

He's very kind to her?

Denise: No, he thinks she doesn't have good values.

He belittles her values?

Denise: Yes, because she has to have designer clothes and she should be studying all the time. Yes, he has very high standards.

He has high standards. Now, is this something you're saying or something he's saying? Do you feel Allan has high values?

Denise: Very much, he's responsible.

To what?

Denise: If he says he's going to do something, he does it.

That's clear.

Denise: He was a cub scout leader. He works for the council and then goes to meetings.

Stephen: He's a good father.

Denise: He'll go to the park and fly a kite.

With who?

Denise: He did with my son and with my daughter. He was a good father. He thinks they should be studying all the time.

So he has high values.

Denise: He talks about table manners and reading and vocabulary. All these things are so important to him.

Are they important to you?

Denise: Saying "hello" to a neighbor and using his name.

Those are nice things. I'm trying to understand something though. Are you telling me —just so I understand, Denise — that you feel Allan has high values and, in an overall sense, you would classify him as a good family man?

Denise: Yes.

But he drove away your son and he drove away Mark.

Denise: And my mother also, now.

And he drove away your mother. And he's driving you away.

Denise: Because he's unhappy. He doesn't love me. I want to fix him.

You want to fix him in order to avoid being alone.

Denise: I don't like him to be suffering like this.

Is that right?

Denise: Yes.

That's very kind, but he's not so kind to you. He's violent and he threatens you. He's angry most of the time, a lot of the time, yes?

Denise: Yes.

And there's something you're carrying from the past that, at this point, you don't feel you can forgive him for.

Denise: Yes.

But you want to stay with him because it is safer than being alone.

Denise: I think that maybe if I had a good job I would have left. But I haven't worked in several years.

He wouldn't support you if you left?

Denise: I think he would, but he's a teacher.

So it's not a very lucrative situation.

Denise: And Crawfield County's very expensive.

So part of this is economic.

Denise: Yes.

It's hard to leave. It's economically difficult for you to leave. How big a factor is that?

Denise: It's big.

It's big, an understandable factor, and so now you're adding another dimension to this — not just the loneliness, but you're not sure you could survive without him.

Denise: Yes.

I understand why it is logical in this context to try to fix him. That is an understandable solution on the basis of the situation you described to me. It's so difficult to leave. Economic survival is hard in Crawfield County and you've never been alone. That's all understandable and so to fix him somehow would be the best solution. How do you go about fixing Allan? How do you stop Allan from being violent?

Denise: I think I can't.

I don't know how. If you were nicer to him, do you think he would be less violent?

Denise: I tried that for a couple weeks.

It didn't work.

Denise: It didn't work.

If you did everything he says, would he be less violent?

Denise: If I become invisible and quiet and stay away from him completely; if I went to work every day, everything would be fine. That's what he said.

He said that? If you got a job, he'd shape up?

Denise: "Get a job, get a job," yeah. And when I had a job, he said, "Get a real job." He was never happy.

But what you're saying to me is that if you isolated yourself from him, he wouldn't be violent. If you kind of snuck around in some invisible way.

Denise: I do, a lot.

And is he violent? Does he still get angry?

Denise: Yes.

So that doesn't work either, does it?

Denise: Nothing will.

And so, what I hear you saying is that the man you're living with, in your mind, whether it's true or not, is somewhat dangerous. When he corners you, you take off your glasses.

Denise: Yes.

Because you're pretty sure you're going to get hit, right?

Denise: Right.

And he's locked you in a dark place?

Denise: No, there's a living room down there.

Oh, all right. But he's locked you downstairs?

Denise: Yes.

He's done all the other things we've mentioned. And you've tried to be nice and he's still this way. And you've tried to do everything he wants and he's still that way.

Denise: Right.

So whatever you do on the level of behavior doesn't seem to have any effect on whether he's violent or not. So you figure if he got spiritual, this would end, if he read the same books you read.

Denise: Yes, if he'd listen to tapes or do yoga with me.

He'd get less violent.

Denise: Yes.

But he won't do those things.

Denise: A little bit.

And the little bit, does it seem to be making him less violent?

Denise: I don't know yet.

Okay, this is your hope, isn't it Denise?

Denise: Oh, yes.

This is it. We're right into the place....

Denise: Even if I left, I would want him to like himself.

You hope somehow that if he could adopt your spirituality, he would lose this anger.

Denise: Yes.

Yes, so people who pick up spirituality don't get angry or they lose an anger that they're having trouble dealing with. Is that the way you see it — that spirituality has something to do with getting rid of anger?

Denise: Yes, not using it out loud.

Not using anger out loud is one of the reasons people become spiritual.

Denise: When you're spiritual you can look at things differently.

And you don't get angry.

Denise: I still get angry sometimes.

Do you?

Denise: Yes, and he yells at me and says, "How can you be angry if you're reading A Course in Miracles? *Why don't you see things differently?"*

Right, right. But you're saying that one of the purposes of *A Course in Miracles* is to assist someone who is very angry in not being very angry.

Denise: No, it's only for me.

That's the purpose of it for you?

Denise: No, the Course *is for me. I can't do anything for anybody else.*

Right, but I'm saying that when a person takes up the *Course*, if Allan took up the *Course*, one of the effects might be that he would stop being angry?

Denise: Yes.

So you're saying that someone whose anger is sometimes at a dangerous level might be helped by spirituality or *A Course in Miracles*.

Denise: Right.

That's one of the reasons someone might become spiritual is to deal with dangerous anger.

Denise: Right.

And that's one of the hopes you have in dealing with Allan's anger.

Denise: Just to feel that there's something else in the world.

Besides?

Denise: His aloneness.

He's lonely?

Denise: I think so. If he plays chess at work, he comes home and says, "Guess what I did? I played chess at lunchtime." — like I have to give him a gold star and say, "Isn't that wonderful!"

He's kind of childlike in that respect.

Denise: Yeah, and when somebody calls him, he goes to play tennis during the summer.

He feels light?

Denise: Yeah.

Does he seem to like it when you like him?

Denise: I.... no, no matter what I do, it's not good.

But when he comes home from playing chess and you kind of give him a gold star, he likes that, yes?

Denise: If he takes out the garbage, he needs a gold star. I have to run to the door to greet him. I'm supposed to put out his clothes in the morning and polish his shoes.

Is that literal?

Denise: No, if I was a good wife, I would put his clothes out.

You'd also be working.

Denise: And I'd also be working, yes. And I would get up and make his breakfast. He leaves at seven and I don't get up. I asked him months ago, I said, "Okay, I will get up if you'd like me to get up and make breakfast," and he said, "It's twenty years too late."

Twenty years too late meaning he's given up. You're not a good servant.

Denise: In the last couple of months — he's been off work for two or three weeks — I do make his breakfast.

And why do you do that, Denise, just out of curiosity, why do you do that?

Denise: I cook all day. I make lentil soup, I make brown rice, I'm chopping vegetables. Three times a week, I'm cooking big.

Right, and you do that for yourself?

Denise: For myself, for him, for my daughter, for company.

Does he appreciate it?

Denise: Not really, but he'd miss it if it was gone.

Right, that's interesting. He doesn't appreciate it, at least in terms of your statement. But if you took it away from him, it would be a reason to abuse you.

Denise: I went to Florida in January for a month. And when I came home he said, "I didn't miss you when you were gone. I want you to leave." This is what started it.

And at that moment you didn't leave because you were too afraid to leave.

Denise: No, I said, "If you're so unhappy with your job and with me and with everything, I will leave in October." And I wrote down what I wanted, that he could have the house and I would take the money.

What money?

Denise: The CD's that were coming due in October. I wrote it all down and he would give me $200 a week so I could get an apartment, and then two days later I changed my mind. I said, "What am I doing?" I wrote it down differently. I said that I want the house and he could take all the money. I don't want any support. I'll live on my little disability. I just want the house. I don't want to lose my daughter. And then he said, "You've changed your mind. How could you do that?" He said, "It's my house and I'm not leaving." He said, "I'll burn it down first."

Now this is a man with high values.

Denise: Yes.

This is a man who would burn his house down to prevent his wife from keeping her child, is that right?

Denise: Right.

This is the high values that we're....I mean, I understand that another side exists, but I want to clarify a rather ambiguous picture here. It's unclear to me, Denise, whether you idolize your husband or whether you hate him. It's not clear to me right now.

Denise: I think I probably hate him.

That's in there, isn't it?

Denise: Definitely, because I'm not giving him what he wants.

You hate him because you're not giving him what he wants.

Denise: No, I'm not giving him what he wants.

I feel such warmth for you. All this concerns me because there's a kind of pattern in this that is fairly typical of abusive situations. And I'm concerned. He isn't getting less abusive, he's getting more so.

Denise: Right.

And he's hit you in the last few months.

Denise: Right.

And you're feeling a kind of dependency on him, and sometimes, in that dependency, you almost idealize him while underneath there's a lot of resentment and even hatred. You're being pulled in two directions at once, isn't that right?

Denise: That's right.

You speak of your husband as a family man with high ideals, high morals, high standards, but he is also threatening you with violence and abusing you in other ways. Do you feel this might be somewhat dangerous?

Denise: Yes.

You feel the possibility of that.

Denise: Yes.

He could hurt you.

Denise: Yes.

I want to support you more than anything I could say to you right now. But I think it's important for you, Denise, to see the pattern here, just to get a look at it — not necessarily to do anything about it — but to get a look at it. Part of you is willing to fade into a kind of fantasy regarding this man, to ignore an aspect of your actual experience with him. That, coupled with a very serious concern about loneliness and economics, creates a danger for you. That's an environment right there that I think other people could identify. My concern for you is that if you don't feel a little anger, you're not going to do anything. I'm very concerned that you might become passive. You've had a hard life. It's been tough and he has been rough. I have a concern for you personally. Do you hear that?

Denise: Yes, I do.

And do you agree with me or do you think I'm off the wall?

Denise: I agree with you.

He could be dangerous.

Denise: Yes.

He could hurt you. There's some evidence of that. Do you feel that I'm with you, Denise?

Denise: Yes, definitely. I'm totally with you.

I think that it's important for you to dismantle any fantasy you have about this man. I mean the lists of how good he is and how charming he is and how high his values are, etc., are all, I'm sure, partially correct. But I think it's important for you to begin to observe the other side of this situation. It has a physical hazard as well as an emotional one.

Where do you find yourself at this point right now, in regard to our dialogue? Where do you find yourself?

Denise: With a lot of things to think about and a lot of hope.

Good, what are the things you would like to think about?

Denise: Oh, I'd like to look at Allan and see him the way he is and how I fantasize him.

You do recognize that you have been doing that?

Denise: Yes, and I will not back off. And if he yells or acts up, I'll stay right there and see what he does. He doesn't like to threaten me.

But if he....

Denise: And if he becomes abusive, I'll just have to tell my daughter that I have my own pride and I'm going to have to find my own apartment. And if he does hit me, I will call the police and have him put out.

Okay.

Denise: I just don't want to do battle. I guess I like him on some level and I don't want to take everything away from him that he's saved and worked for all these years.

Well, you've been part of that though, haven't you?

Denise: He's the one who says it's all his.

Yes, but he says a lot of things to you. What about you? Weren't you part of what he saved and worked for all these years? It's just him?

Denise: He handed me his paycheck every two weeks. It goes in the checking account and I pay the bills.

Sure.

Denise: And the money I save now is my disability.

No, but what he's worked and saved for all of his life has nothing to do with you? This is a one-sided ship where you're just a piece of extraneous material? It's been his saving and working all these years and you've had no part of that?

Denise: In his mind.

In his mind, yes.

Denise: In his mind, it's his house.

You see the reason that I feel you are prone to being hurt in this, Denise, is precisely because of the kind of exchange we're having in which what he thinks becomes your truth. Whatever he thinks about you is true. That makes you prone to his violence. Do you understand why I say that?

Denise: Yeah.

His beliefs are yours, no matter what they are. He tells you it's his money; it's his money. He tells you that you gave him a bad baby and it's true; you had a bad baby and you're wrong. It seems to me that you're prone to believing that whatever he says is true and that's a setup.

(Silence)

What's going through you in the silence?

Denise: I never thought that he was violent.

No? It never occurred to you that, for instance, what happened with Mark was not violent?

Denise: I never thought that was violent.

Does it occur to you now that it might be violent?

Denise: Yes.

And his locking you in the basement or being angry at you for whatever you do — you've never thought of that as violence? I'm just interested.

Denise: I thought that was how an angry person acts.

An angry person acts violent sometimes.

Denise: I didn't think of it as being something dangerous.

But you said you even take off your glasses when he comes near because you're prepared to be hit. You said you're afraid of him all of the time. If you're not afraid of danger, what are you afraid of?

Denise: I didn't think it was serious danger.

Well, I don't know that it is serious danger. Do you think it might be?

Denise: It's come up so many times.

He's done it too many times, is that what you're saying?

Denise: Yes.

Is that by way of saying that it might be serious danger?

Denise: It probably is serious.

It's something to be concerned about at any rate, wouldn't you think?

Denise: Yes, but I never worried before.

You never were really concerned up until now?

Denise: Right.

But how did that tally with the fact that you've been afraid of him since the day you met him?

Denise: I'm afraid to say the wrong thing.

And if you say the wrong thing, what happens?

Denise: He explodes.

Right, and that explosion is dangerous or not dangerous?

Denise: He pulls my hair sometimes.

He's done that?

Denise: Oh, many times.

He pulls your hair. Is that violent?

Denise: He doesn't beat me up. I never had black eyes or broken arms.

Denise, he pulls your hair and he locks you in the basement and he hits you in the face. Isn't that right?

Denise: Yes, and he punched me.

That's not beating you up? You mean you've got to be black and blue?

Denise: Yes.

Before you're a victim of violence?

Denise: Right.

Do you think that's true?

Denise: Probably not, I never thought I was a victim of violence.

Well, let me ask you this. If Allan took Louise, pulled her hair, punched her in the face, exploded, cornered her and locked her in the basement, would he be safe as a father?

Denise: No.

So why is he safe as a husband?

Denise: Because he gives me his paycheck.

That's understandable. In other words, this is the price you pay. This is the price you pay for being economically secure.

Denise: Yes.

That's a political problem and I understand it, I really do. And you meant that, didn't you — when you were down to the nitty gritty — that if someone gave you $50,000 tomorrow, you'd be gone, wouldn't you?

Denise: I wouldn't go with $50,000. I'd go with more than that. It wouldn't be enough.

Well does this CD you're talking about amount to more than that?

Denise: Yes.

I'm concerned because by not calling his behavior violent, you are setting yourself up for something difficult. You keep excusing him by saying that he is a good man, but unhappy. You keep hoping to save him, change him and help him in some way. Then it becomes your problem.

Denise: Yes.

He's got someone to hit and he's got someone who tries to make him happy. I'd forget all the unconditional love stuff. I'd drop it right in the ditch because I think you have something to deal with straight off that has nothing to do with unconditional love. It has to do with self-respect.

Denise: I know that, and when I'm not afraid, I think I should be afraid. It's comfortable to be afraid.

It's comfortable to be afraid. When you're not afraid of what, of leaving?

Denise: Of leaving, or of him leaving.

Right, when you're not afraid — now this is important— when you're not afraid of leaving, you think there's something wrong because you should be afraid.

Denise: Yes.

Who tells you you should be afraid of leaving? Whose idea is that?

Denise: It's mine.

Based on what?

Denise: I don't know — based on I'm probably still a little afraid.

He knows you're afraid of leaving, doesn't he?

Denise: Yes.

He must know. He plays hardball with your fear. He plays it for all it's worth. Don't you think that's true?

Denise: Yes.

He's aware that you're afraid of leaving, so he can threaten you. That's abusive. Just snap it into where it hurts — put you out on the street, take your house away, take your daughter.

Denise: I don't know. I feel like I have to find somebody else to take me away.

Stephen: Yeah, I know.

Denise: And that's what I feel and I don't want that.

That's beautiful, that's beautiful. You feel that you have to find some other dependency before you can give up this one. I understand that. If you could only find someone else to latch onto the way you latched onto him — only this someone will treat you better — then you can make the shift, yes?

Denise: Yes.

You see yourself as a rag doll. I'm not saying that's the only way you see yourself, but that's part of it. He pulls your hair. He throws you in the basement, punches you in the face. I don't think of you that way. I don't feel you that way. I don't see you that way. Do you hear what I'm saying, Denise?

Denise: Yes.

When you spoke about Mark I could feel the mother love in your heart. It was so strong, so pure. What you did was very courageous. Do you understand that? You did what you saw to be the best thing in a very pressured circumstance. That's a hell of a thing to be able to do — to give up your son under those conditions. I really think it's remarkable. It wasn't easy. You did what you had to do and, in the end, you helped your son. He's in a beautiful home. Unfortunately you can't be acknowledged for this when articles appear in the paper. But you did get him that beautiful home. I really admire that.

But I'm concerned for you. I think the violence has to be taken seriously.

Denise: I know you're right.

It's been escalating. It hasn't been diminishing. That concerns me too. How do you feel right now, Denise? Is it numb, or do you feel something?

Denise: My legs feel numb, but I feel like I have a better chance of seeing things clearly when I go home.

I didn't disturb you too much?

Denise: No, not at all. I think I was so afraid of going home and everything being the same.

Yes, I understand that.

Denise: I feel that I can maybe see things the way they are.

Do you feel complete, Denise? Be very honest with me. Do you feel complete on our journey together? I'm willing to go on, so I want to know if you feel complete.

Denise: I don't know what that means.

I mean, do you feel that you and I have had contact, exchange, that you've moved in some way?

Denise: Yes, I feel like I've learned so much.

And that you're not up against the same wall that you were up against before we started?

Denise: No, I feel like I can look at things differently, and take my time and make changes this year.

Do you have someone in your life who you can call and speak to specifically about this situation? Someone who is not involved and has no particular interest at heart except supporting you?

Denise: My girlfriends give me advice, but mostly, "He's a good man," "You shouldn't leave," "You shouldn't get in a position of...."

So you don't have anyone to support you.

Denise: They give me the opposite.

Right. Now I don't want an answer right away, but I would really like to know — and people just look in their hearts for this — if there's someone who would offer Denise an ear on the telephone or in person whenever she needs it, who will take a supportive role in relation to this, preferably somebody who understands what she's up against.

Mary: I would.

Carol: So would I.

Can you accept this, Denise — that there are some people who would give you their telephone numbers and say yes, unequivocally, to your calling them, night or day, when you need strength to get through this?

Denise: Yes, thank you. It's so beautiful, Stephen. I really believe it. Thank you everyone. Thank you, Stephen.

THE NEXT DAY

I had a very definite sense that there were two rivers running through you in terms of the way you perceived what was going on in your life. A contradicted B and B contradicted A and yet you had the capacity or the desire — or you felt the necessity

—to hold onto both of them because you didn't want to scrap either one. At the same time you were afraid to discount his in a certain way, and so you were carrying them both. And when we got to the story of Mark, it became increasingly clear that you were carrying Allan's story and your story but the gap between them — the emotional gap between his version and your version — was so great that it was creating a kind of fiery problem inside you. It made you numb.

Last night you were able to come right down into the heart of the contradiction, stay with it, take a look at it and then begin to acknowledge and honor your story as yours and his story as his. And I think that's the mission ahead. It isn't so much a matter of preoccupying yourself with a defensive posture or negating his story. I don't think it would be wise to go back home and engage him in a sustained argument. Such an approach would be dangerous and not productive for either of you. I think that it's important for your focus to be on honoring and acknowledging your vision.

You weren't carrying both stories because you're a confused person. You were carrying both stories because you were nobly attempting to do what can't be done — to accommodate a very depressing contradiction in points of view about the very same thing. You were trying to carry two things at once. It was an attempt to reconcile. It was an attempt at non-violence and I think it's beautiful. But I think you're going to learn that real strength is a higher form of non-violence, a more effective form of non-violence — and that is self-acceptance.

Denise: Thank you so much.

Thank you, Denise. I think you can notice too that we were using content to transcend content. I mean there was content, but there was something else between us that was going on other than the content of your parable as it unfolded. There was something more than the content. There was the communal experience of joining through that content and then transcending it.

John: I don't think you could have stayed with it so long if that hadn't been true.

That's right, that's right. If it were simply content and that was the level that we were on, it would have fallen into the realm of ordinary conversation, of a person telling their troubles. And that would have been fine, but it wouldn't have had the depth and the remarkable transformative qualities that Denise brought to it as a result of her willingness to communicate with me.

Denise: It didn't feel more than twenty minutes to me.

Yes, it was almost three hours. It's interesting, Denise, that you have been in a difficult spot with your feelings and your relationship to this situation for a long, long time. It's gotten coiled up, bunched up in various ways. And it's very rare — and this is something we can all agree with and it's not a puffed-up statement — it's very rare to find someone who is willing to see you through, and this group saw you through.

Denise: This has been incredible for me. I came here with a lot of fear. And I think I fell off the mountain. I know I did. And the pain was beautiful. And I know my whole life has changed because I feel the Holy Spirit came through Stephen into my heart. I was blind before and I didn't even know I was blind. And I know when I leave here I'm never going to see the way I saw before. And I'm never going to accept things the way they were. I know things are going to change drastically. And I've never felt such love and support. I want to thank everybody. And I always felt very happy and I thought I had everything. I mean I didn't have to work. I went to classes. I painted. I did yoga. I meditated. You know, it was a beautiful life. I had a massage twice a week. And it was because I was alone and I didn't know I was alone. I had to keep running and running. And now I'm excited, I'm really excited, to go home and to sit with myself and to work through everything. And I know it's going to be very positive for my daughter and probably for my husband, and I think I'm tired of making believe we have a happy family — that's what my mother-in-law said.

And I feel just such love for everyone and I feel like I'm in the place that's the place to be. I didn't know people could live in a place like this or have a family like this. And I was, I guess, happy with pain. I was comfortable with pain and I would miss it if it went away. I never felt joy like this and I want to keep this joy forever. And I love you, Stephen, so much. Thank you so much. Thank you everyone.

Thank you.

10

**When the mind is clear,
it is experienced
as space.**

Andrew: The practice that I learned from you several years ago and that I have been doing steadily seems to have undergone an evolution. I'd like to tell you about it and see what your reaction is.

I remember that my experience for a long time was feeling the feelings in the body and then going back to thought. As soon as I realized I had become absorbed in thoughts, I would return my attention to the bodily experience. I did it like that for a long time. Although it was always effective and I noticed movement, I sensed something to be missing for me.

What I have discovered lately is that I need to pay attention to the thoughts, but on a very conscious level. When I found myself in thought before, it was semi-submerged. I didn't know what the thoughts were saying. To go to them took away from the experience of the feeling.

I often wondered about where was the tendency of the feeling. As I have been really paying attention lately to what the thoughts are saying on a conscious level, I find myself feeling more intensely. For a period of time, at first, I was conflicted because the practice, as I had been doing it, was very good for me and I didn't want to subvert something that was so good.

I find that the attention on thought makes some room for the feeling. I don't dwell on what the thought is saying, but it is important for me to know what it is saying before I go back to the feeling.

Do you understand what I am saying?

You don't let the thoughts become unconscious. You stay aware of what the message is that they are offering to you.

Andrew: There were so many times when I found myself so immersed in thought that I didn't even know I was thinking until I became aware suddenly that that's where I was. Everything that was running through my thoughts was not very conscious.

It seems like because my thoughts were not very conscious, I always had to go back to them, like a rubber band. I had to go back to thinking, like a magnet. When I really pay attention to the thoughts on a conscious level and discover what they are saying, I don't seem to go back to the same thoughts all the time.

I understand that and I don't think it's at all out of line with what we have been talking about in these circles across the years. The practice is so loose to start with. It's not a doctrine or a dogma. It has no preordained setup. It is based entirely on understanding and compassion.

Andrew: I used to hope that if I removed myself from the thoughts altogether that they would eventually be less important and maybe not as present.

Many times thoughts arise in such a way that they have a high impact on our feeling experience, but the thought doesn't actually appear consciously. In that foggy unconsciousness, the thought has gained a greater grip on our feelings because it can't even be examined intellectually. Because we don't know what the thought/belief actually is, it can have a different kind of power over us.

You are speaking about a nonjudgmental or nonevaluative observation of what is going on within you. This makes sense. The practice we talk about in this work evolves out of an understanding. Therefore, if the understanding is intact, the practice isn't a law. The stark presentation of the practice in my teaching role draws attention to the dichotomy between the thought and the feeling.

It may be helpful, at this point, for you to pay attention to the content of thought. That is different, however, from believing that the content and the feeling are the same. You are offering yourself a chance to examine the propaganda. It is important to recognize that most of our thoughts spring from conditioning. Our thoughts and concerns represent a kind of recapitulation of childhood events. Looking at them reveals the tone of our personal history.

This non-evaluative observation breaks a habit. Being aware of the distortion that belief and thought bring disempowers them. It takes some of the charge out and gives greater strength to the feeling, to the energy.

When we are having submerged, inhibiting thoughts that are not available to us consciously, they constantly cut into the feeling. Sometimes by noticing what we are actually saying to ourselves, what we believe, there is an opportunity for a new start.

Christopher: When we are talking about the thought and feeling, I am wondering if you could clarify the distinction between body sensation, thought and feeling? When we go to the body and feel, are we dealing with body vibrations, tightness, contractions, etc.? Are we really talking about feelings or emotions on that level?

Most of the time people are not talking about feelings at all. This is an important observation especially in relationship to deep, energetic communication like healing therapy.

Ninety-nine percent of the time, at least at the outset, feelings are not being discussed. What is being discussed is physical tension and the way that tension is cutting off the energetic, body vibration through the imposition of false meanings.

What we are calling feeling, much of the time, is the conscious experience of a squeeze between physical tension, the impulse of life current, a wounded feeling experience in the background and the commentary of thought. Often, even when the conscious thought is disengaged from the so-called feeling, we are still dealing with a residue of tension in the body.

Part of our work is a graceful three-step movement. This movement is not linear, but we might be able to grasp it at first if it is presented in a linear way. It's vital to understand in working with ourselves or with someone else that the first movement toward the body is usually a movement toward tension. When we disengage from the oppression of routine thought, our first experience is not necessarily going to be release, because the response of the physical body is habituated to contraction even after the thought is transcended.

The body remains caught in a particular position. When the body's position ceases to press as hard against the feeling, something begins to arise which resembles a pure energetic tone, but it's not exactly the same. At first, we might come to a kind of bruise which is the result of holding the body in a certain way for so long. The effect of the resistance and the defense can be mistaken for the feeling itself. We are certainly closer to the energy tone at this point, but it may hurt or feel vulnerable in a particularly delicate way.

If we stay with the bruise long enough, we come to the wound. It is the wound which we had been defending and protecting all along. At the bottom of all this, is the pure feeling — the wave. That wave, that pulsation of current is very different from the layers of meaning and tension which had obscured it in the past.

We sometimes hurt on the inside. This hurt is interpreted by the conditioned mind as a signal to turn against our own internal experience. We begin to layer our feelings with fog. It is important to see the precision of this in working with ourselves or with someone else. We can understand why it requires such patience to enter into this kind of healing process.

When we assume ourselves to be talking about feelings, we are probably talking more about the experience of not permitting feelings to emerge, and all the symptoms that creates. When the turn toward the pure feeling is actually accomplished, we experience an urge to create. The scope of possibilities widens. This creativity can even begin to manifest as a dissatisfaction with current conditions, as a kind of restlessness.

For a period of time, as we delve deeply, we may have to sit with a surge of creativity and an inhibition — to feel this interplay in a physical way and to observe the tendency of mind to create a story line which distracts us from moving ahead.

Feelings feed the visible body and the subtle body as well. They are also an impetus to create. Feelings seek to nurture and express. Energies enter into the body in a conscious way. They nourish the body and, as a result of the overflow that comes from being nourished, the body is able to share some of its energy through the creative act. Creativity is an ecological return. It is giving back that which we have taken in.

At very subtle levels, in a most delicate physical terrain, we have all been injured. As life current passes into those injured places, we experience pain. The pure feeling is not consciously available to us at that moment. The pain has a greater impact on our attention than does the feeling itself.

When the pain dominates our attention, the feeling can not be consciously experienced in a clear way. Our sensitivity to the vibratory tone has been diminished. We feel instead the heaviness of pain. When subtle body pain flashes into consciousness, the conditioned mind interprets that signal as an indication that something is wrong. It seeks blame, insight, ideas, explanations and generally deals with this important message by turning against it.

The container-mind invents a panicky label, a vague or conflicted description of what's going on, and the body acts as the slave to that description by shutting down. It pulls its weight toward suppression as opposed to permission, density as opposed to transparency. That movement creates a strange interplay between an evolutionary signal and an attack on the signal by the body and the mind.

The thought attack would have no power if it didn't have the visible habit body as its ally. The body begins to close down on the pain. We end up in a tight relationship to the energetic pulsation which is seeking to feed us and to create through us.

All of this becomes most peculiar, ornate and complex. As thought, physical suppression, woundedness and the underlying energetic pulsation interact in the bodily frame, the mind looks at it all as one thing and not as an interwoven mesh of many elements. It perceives this new experience as a threat and begins to create new stories and myths to explain it. It then begins to attack its own attack, and it is then that we speak of confusion, frustration and heaviness. The mind begins to argue with its own invention.

Such understandings, if they are organic, give rise to a high degree of patience when we are being with ourselves or with someone else. Moving through these layers of confusion or illusion is a refined and delicate process. We can be pretty sure that when someone reveals the difficulty they are having, that a lot of it is thought, and what is being called a feeling is a cluster of several different elements.

Pain is not a threat. It is a call for return and restoration. It is a call for attention. It is not a message that something is wrong. When the word illusion is used in this context, it relates to the way the world looks when filtered through a mirage of suppression, bruising, evolutionary signals, thought, as well as our memories and beliefs. Our life will inevitably be substantially discolored by this mix.

Someone who was listening to a talk the other day told me that she was afraid of letting go of her need to control the outside. As we spoke, it became clear that no one has any control over much of what goes on outside themselves. There is nothing to let go of. We only have control over whether the body is to be used suppressively or expressively.

The mind, as we currently use it, has little or no control over the outside. It may seem that when the body is tight and armored we are exerting some level of influence. But the only control we actually have is whether to make the body tense or whether to say "yes" to life, to Eros.

Compassionate Self-Care involves a basic recognition that we don't have control. We are out on the edge of some great mystery attempting to seek safety and comfort through fantasies of control. As we begin to divest ourselves of those fantasies, a clear understanding begins to emerge that nothing makes sense in the old terms. At that point, all we have left is self-care.

Before we can understand Compassionate Self-Care, before the practice is deeply ingrained, even the idea of God is just a hope or a dream because we have been taught to pray through thoughts. Thoughts can not receive the love or the bliss. Only the body can. Compassionate Self-Care is ultimately a grounded, physiological approach to life which asserts the truth of the frontal membrane and the spiritual reality of our bodily experience.

Compassionate Self-Care also is based on the understanding that what we currently call the mind is a clutter of prejudices and mechanical responses that do not necessarily relate to reality.

We are at the edge. We must be willing to stand there, in a stark place sometimes, and stare into what appears to be an abyss and to wait. The rug is gone, the ladders are down and the escape hatches have disappeared. We stay easy with ourselves, breathe and allow the attention to be with the heart. This is self-care.

We are conditioned to relate to each other and to ourselves either with a sentimental stroke or the whip of self-hate. We associate care with coddling and mild dishonesty. Rarely do we associate care with absolute directness — staying with it, riding it through, letting the pain go where it will.

The process we speak of here represents a different kind of care from what we would get in some breezy self-help approach. It is a process devoted to those who find themselves unable anymore to make sense of a pattern of existence which clings to imaginary beliefs in order to find safety — including spiritual doctrines and ideals.

As we walk into the adventure, into the unknown sphere, the only partner we have is self-care, openness. And the only act available to us then is learning how to use the body as a doorway and not as a wall.

We can't be fiddling with ideologies and practicing direct, unsentimental self-care as well. This process is based on absolute poverty and simplicity in relationship to overlays and ideas. We come to ourselves over and over again, not knowing anything.

To look for the truth we must turn toward mystery. The conceptual mind can not locate truth. It can not find the depth or the open space. There is no truth in ideas, beliefs, scripture or religion. There is truth only in the sacred mystery. At best, the beliefs and the ideas, the great scriptural works, which have come to us from the past, function as inspiration. But for the journey to actually begin, they must be put down.

In some ways psychology mystifies our experience. It doesn't mention where experience is taking place. The first question anyone should ask a therapist before beginning a shared work is, "Where is my experience taking place? Where am I having my experience?" We must know where our experience is taking place; otherwise what are we going to work on; what are we trying to heal?

Real experience is taking place in the body. If healing is to come, we must turn to the body. This doesn't mean we ignore what is going on in the head, but we must recognize that the true experience of life is taking place somewhere else. Life passes through the heart as wave upon wave of mysterious phenomena. The eyes open into the front of the body and not into the structure of thought.

The human being can not be explained. But if we want to create a poetic description, it can at least be said that the core of our being is in and around the heart. A human being is a specific radiant pulsation of energy which is located in a body. The particular body through which that pulsation expresses, is, in a sense, designed for that particular tone or pulsation. The human being is a radiant pulsation and the body is a receiver, transformer and amplifier of that pulsation.

A radiance accompanies the body. In an imagistic way, we might say that the radiance has a center. It is like the web of a spider. The spider lives at the very center of its own emanating matrix. At the center is the physical body and surrounding it is a nearly imperceptible, but elegantly geometric, web. At the center of the center is the heart, the solar plexus, and the area around the heart.

When we seek help from someone who assumes that the identity is a series of voices in the head or some version of that, how can we be healed? The real healing involves the repair and restoration of the radiant web around the body and its delicate emanations. Healing is not the repair of thought.

The torment of all neurosis and other psychological difficulties is physical pain. A secondary aspect of the physical pain is the mind's attempt to explain or even to create ritualistic, magical solutions to that which hurts. The healer assists in leading someone to the breath, the body and the being within and around the physical core. The rest, in a sense, takes care of itself.

Andrew: It's so deeply ingrained sometimes that it almost seems hopeless.

What you are saying is very important. The healer who can stay in touch with hopelessness, not cynicism, bitterness or negativity, can have a much greater impact than a person who is filled with ideas and plans.

Our work is to reveal space and not to get somewhere. We don't aim towards a categorical goal, but instead we wait for openings, hints and indications. The purpose of a deep healing work does not involve linear, psychological goals. It involves translating experience as it is into spaciousness and mystery. We leave behind the confined context of counterfeit space we live in so much of the time.

If we picture a most intricate and elaborate spider web and then imagine that someone has stuck their finger into it, twisted it around a bit and caused tangles or breaks, we gain some sense of what wounding looks like in the subtle body. Maybe we can envision pieces of leaf or twig hanging from the web at various points, disrupting the pure geometric harmony. It is this and the mind's description which give rise to what is called neurosis.

Attention is a healing force, but not a force of aggression or intervention. It is like fertilizer, compost. We put it on or around the plant and some catalytic process occurs which brings new growth. The healing process is a particular use of the attention.

Christopher: When you were talking about healing, you brought up the problem of pain. I have a sense that if you can allow the erotic energy to rise in the body without seeking a release, that can be a breakthrough to healing. That particular energy has a power that others don't have.

I would only add here that there isn't any energy but erotic energy. There is Eros, life, and it is pouring through us. We are receiving it as loneliness, sex, desire, hate, etc., but it's all Eros.

Christopher: That's interesting. I can see in what I just said that basically I must just discover the one energy. I may feel it as my sex drive, but it is just the one energy. There is a way in which we tend to try to release that Eros before it has arisen all the way. I sometimes just go for the release, to try to get away from it.

The notion of release as healing is a misunderstanding. Healing is not about release; it is about digestion. We let the life current feed us. The notion of release is based on the assumption that there are negative and positive things within us. We release the negative and keep the positive. Healing is not about release and getting rid of something. It is about transmutation. It is a kind of alchemy in which density is transformed into light through a purification in the fires of the heart.

Healing is so much more beautiful than working out issues. It's so much more exotic than that. There are no issues. Or we might say there are and there are not issues. If you are attached to one end of the system, issues seem very real. At the other end, there are no issues to work out at all.

The individual is a pulsation with a particular tone and frequency. It has a radiant center. Surrounding that center is a matrix which is made up of echoing movements of energy which can be compared to the waves created by a rock thrown into a still pool. Those waves, the emanating webs, are hollow. Energies stream from the cosmos and pour into the hollowness of the web. They come to certain openings in the visible body. They come to the frontal membrane. This membrane breathes just like the lungs. It opens and closes in regular rhythmic intervals.

As the frontal membrane opens, it takes in that which is moving through the hollowness in the matrix surrounding the body, and as it closes, those energies begin to digest. They ascend through the form and nourish it. When the membrane opens again, it lets out that which it had once taken in, only now in a different form, and takes more in again.

Most of us are not experiencing a pure rhythm in the opening and closing of the frontal membrane. It has been jammed or congested because the body is being used as a wall.

Often an event which shocks, positive or negative, forces the body to open so that congested energies in the outer web suddenly flood the body. This can be very inspiring or terribly frightening.

The reason we return to the breathing when such openings occur is because an intricate relationship exists between the gross physical event of breathing and the subtle event in which energies are moved into the body. When breathing is allowed to be rhythmic and conscious, then the breathing of the subtle body begins to restore its balance.

Sometimes the big hits in life give us the greatest evolutionary potential. Because of the disruption caused by crisis, we have the chance to let go of limiting interpretations and enter into the subtle body breathing with a new openness. If we don't get punched once in a while, really moved on some level, the habit-force, the contraction gets more deeply entrenched. Our reality myth takes on an increasing strength. The value of crisis is that it forces the body to open and if we know how to work with that opening, we can begin to feed ourselves with the flood of energy that inevitably comes through.

Lynn: I have had, since I was a kid, a very violent temper that would erupt at extremely erratic moments. For a period of time, I was in intensive therapy to deal with this. It is shocking to me that I still have this.

The most abusive part of the anger has gone away, but I still find that, occasionally, vestiges of this off-the-wall anger will return. There is so much force with it that it destroys trust that had been carefully built up. It happens maybe once every six months. It comes when I am feeling vulnerable and it just happens. This is an area of my life that I hate.

There is something in what you have just been speaking about that seems relevant. It never happens with anyone except those I really care about. Is this part of the habit or what?

I could give you an outrageous explanation for what is going on, but I don't want it to become an abstraction.

Lynn: At this point in time, it is somewhat abstract because I am not feeling it right now. But I do feel that understanding would help.

Then I'll offer this. Please do with it what you will. Your body, our bodies, are a very complex system of circuitry, as we've discussed. The circuitry, for the most part, surrounds the visible, physical form.

Energies move through the field around the body, into the body and then are transformed and expressed. The body, in a balanced state, is opening and closing in regular rhythms.

Each individual has a different relationship to energy. Some people are very intense, with high charges and strong impulses. Other people have a different way of expressing their relationship to life current. You are a person with a high charge. You experience an intensity of energy.

As the life current begins to pass through the circuitry, the field around the body, it is transformed or individualized by your body in very intense ways. It doesn't become diffuse.

Some people diffuse energy as it comes and others concentrate it. You are a person who concentrates it. That concentrated energy comes through the field around your body and meets a close-down somewhere. It is blocked at the gate.

Just as there would be in an electrical system, a close-down creates a build-up of charge. There is a build-up of charge behind the gate, the close-down. The passage of energy can not be completed in a full way so there is a build-up of charge. If that gate were suddenly opened, the build-up would come gushing through like a force. This force is then personalized.

A soft feeling of love for someone, being at the edge of a melt, suddenly opens the gate for you. In the most intimate of encounters, the guard comes down and the built-up charge floods through the gate and courses through the body. Because of a habit of fear and a personalizing tendency in general, this event seems dangerous and is turned toward the other person. All the energy gets pushed out toward your friend.

This whole event has no psychological meaning. There was a build-up of charge, a huge surge, a personalization of that surge and then an attack. This is what you are experiencing in those circumstances.

The process of recovery, if you will, involves a more balanced relationship to your intensity, so that it doesn't get stuffed back. You are a person who intensifies and concentrates energy and therefore it can't be held back for too long without a breakthrough. That breakthrough is not caused by someone who challenges you because you know so well how to tighten against that. It comes rather as a result of someone who opens you, softens you, because the guard is dropped.

Unless both parties have some understanding of this, it is taken personally, understandably so. But it isn't personal at all. Someone put the key in the lock and this is what comes pouring out when the door is opened.

Your experience is an electrical discharge in accordance with the intensity of your character. It is an evolutionary workout. Something massive comes through a conducting element, but that element is not quite ready to accommodate it. We could look at your experience as a psychological problem, and of course, headway might be made that way. But this force is not really about psychology at all. It explodes into the psychological level and appears on that level as well as on many others.

Lynn: This is very provocative. I can't even imagine hearing this before.

Even your language in describing this experience indicated your understanding of it on an energetic level. You spoke of it as a force coming through you which impelled you to do things you didn't want to do.

Lynn: The only thing is that it's ugly.

Only the behavior is ugly. From an aesthetic point of view, the behavior is onerous. It's violent and unfair. But that doesn't mean that the force itself is ugly. It only means that your response to it is ugly.

This force comes crashing through and your response to it is violent. The sudden jerk of this energy into the system causes you to react in a particular way. The behavior and the force are not the same thing. The force is stimulating that behavior because of your own conditioning.

Here is another angle: the reason we close down in the way you describe is because we are afraid to feel something. When someone evokes an opening that part of us does not want to have, then we try to push that person away. The process of full recovery is to open to the energy more consistently and organically so that it doesn't have to explode.

Lynn: This is very helpful.

The force itself is creative and expressive. It is not ugly. When Van Gogh, for instance, entered into that kind of force, he would paint, but at other times, he just couldn't express, and his behavior became disruptive and dangerous to both himself and others.

Lynn: I have had the feeling at times that there is a secret demon within me and I have no idea when it will come out. In that picture, it seems like something is very wrong. What I am hearing you say is different. While it may not be positive, it is workable.

Exactly. With the proper tools, it is workable. It is a daemon, not a demon. It is a non-personal force asking for your surrender. Instead you try to own it. This causes a certain kind of behavior. When we love someone and they love us in return, all the gates begin to break open. That's why we can get so angry at the person we love most dearly. In our love, the supposed safety valves become nonfunctional.

Lynn: God, that's helpful.

Vulnerability is an open door. It is generally experienced after the subtle body breathing has been held down for a long time and then for some reason is opened up again. It creates an odd mixture of fascination and fear. Everything seems raw and dangerous. But vulnerability is an open passageway, a door. It is a signal that the feeling body is trying to correct itself.

Lynn: This makes so much sense because it usually happens after the most magnificent times, right after a peak perfection. That's why it is so scary because it has seemed like a punishment. First there is caring and then this mad behavior. What you are saying is that those occasions open the flood gate in a way that ordinary, tired life couldn't.

Don't you feel something like that force when you are really engaged in your work?

Lynn: Absolutely, but I never have connected the two. I have never revealed this in front of any one. No one would ever know this about me. The connection is very important. It has something to do with my own energy levels.

It has to do with your gift. The real danger of psychology, in its most abstract form, is that it doesn't recognize the electromagnetic nature of life. It functions in a mystical terrain. By ignoring the energetic force, we look for content-laden solutions to pure electrical difficulties. Psychology is really a study of the habit formations which have developed as a result of conditioning. These energies hit the psychology and are colored by it, but they are not caused by the psychology.

Lynn: When I was in therapy, we went back to childhood experiences and looked at fear levels, etc. It was helpful. But what you have just said puts a very different light on it.

Part of the reason that that kind of therapy is helpful is because you sit with someone else and attend to something together. What you explore is secondary to the fact that a healing process is occurring underneath. Do you know what I mean?

Lynn: That's amazing.

In the purest state of a work like this, nothing has to be said. I sit with various people at certain times and we spend an hour in silence. Something extraordinary happens when we do that. It doesn't need an excuse.

All you were doing with the therapist was exploring your body and your fantasies about it. It was the attention that healed. I'm not saying that the understandings weren't useful, but they were secondary to the healing process itself. What is underlying and invisible is always more powerful than what is overriding and visible.

Lynn: This makes sense on a deep level. Even my spiritual work suggested that I should choose to be more loving. But this violent experience would come up after a very intense exchange of love. It always seemed like a spiritual and psychological failure.

The daemon is a force of love. It is one of the forces of love. The behavior is not loving because the force is filtered through various lenses in the psychological realm which have their own limitations. The force is a direction of love.

Lynn: Perhaps now I will be more concerned with the energy and not trying to get rid of it. I will take it differently.

You couldn't get rid of it without crippling yourself, without massive suppression.

Lynn: Very good. Very helpful.

11

The spiritual path is not a
series of cathartic experiences;
it is a movement toward
deep trust and
patient, attentive waiting.

When we speak about spiritual forces or evolutionary forces, we are speaking about forces which are at work in a person all the time even if there is no recognition that such forces exist. At a certain point in time, a recognition may dawn for a particular individual that much more exists in this universe than what appears on the surface. Certain unseen forces and intelligences live within us and around us. At a certain point in our lives, it becomes necessary to cooperate with them in a conscious way.

Cooperation with evolutionary forces involves turning the attention to the heart and disengaging from habitual patterns of thought which define and describe the physical sensations we find there. Such an act creates an environment in which we can begin to consciously cooperate with the unseen forces of life and therefore experience an enhanced sense of support and easiness.

Jon: Does the access come differently to different kinds of people?

Absolutely.

Jon: When you were talking earlier I found the things you were saying interesting, but I was also getting very sleepy, tired, not energized. And then when Rebecca began to talk, I became alive; there was excitement. It seems to me I get places in a dialogic way. You've accessed all this knowledge by yourself. It comes alive for me when someone talks with someone else.

Yes, traditionally breakthroughs from an enclosed space to a greater space are part of a community experience and not necessarily part of an experience which is born in solitude. It's also true, however, that different people respond to different things in different ways. This work is no exception to that. Undoubtedly there's someone here who has been tremendously moved by what I said this morning even though it made you sleepy.

Ruth: I had the opposite experience from what Jon is describing in that I was incredibly moved by the words. They were like mirrors of what was happening inside of me, and then when people spoke I felt like I rose back up to the surface.

That's why I feel the necessity for both ends of this process to be offered — dialogues and talks. Because of where these words come from, and the way they arise, many people who participate feel they are being spoken to directly. I don't know how to explain that phenomenon. But there have always been, in every one of these circles, people who come to me, in just the way that you have, and say that it was as if the words were aimed at them, like there was no one else.

It is important, as part of the work in these circles to notice whatever reaction you may be having and to stay steady with it. It is not necessary to come up to the surface when a dialogue starts or when a talk begins. It's possible to sustain the body as an opening in the midst of different conditions and circumstances. Something other than words goes on here. These words are a reflection of something deeper. Our sitting is a discipline which allows us to practice becoming aware of the invisible energetic level that rides underneath content.

Terri: Oh, wow! What is happening right now is what you're talking about. I felt earlier that if it were possible to express what it felt like, it would come out as some kind of sound, like you'd just shout, feeling like running across a beach and you would yell and yell because it's so big. It's like you can't hold it.

I'm totally with you, Terri. Now, Terri, let's come to the heart together, come to the body, and just allow yourself to be with the body as you are right now. Also allow your attention to be with me. And just tell me what you feel is happening.

Terri: Something is happening.

Can you feel me Terri?

Terri: Oh, yes.

Alice, can you feel this?

Alice: Yes. There's a deep opening.

Lisa: I felt like when you were talking, you were describing very precisely my experience, both the longing and the block, and with it came a sense that I can accept this.

You can accept the fact that both a longing and a block sit inside you.

Lisa: Yes, even though so much of the time it feels like there's something wrong, that I must get past it. I want to be released so much.

But this is very beautiful. What you're saying here now is in the heart of the matter. Each one of us has been taught to characterize a central piece of our existence as a wrongness. What an extraordinary understanding — that a pivotal characteristic of the human condition, the relationship between an unlimited longing, an apparent limit and that which we are longing for has become a source of shame. But there isn't anything else in this life at all. There really isn't anything else. It is odd that we assume, somehow, that we must get over this before we become whole.

All the wisdom bearers who have given so many gifts to humanity were initially motivated by a longing. They followed that longing, learning to respect it as a prayer, rather than fighting with it or trying to make it better. The longing is so innocent. It is everything that this life stands for. There isn't anything else.

Lisa: Oh my goodness, it blows me away.

It's so profoundly important — our hearts long for something; around us are limits and then there is that which transcends those limits, that which we are longing for. Life is a pilgrimage, a simple pilgrimage even though we make it terribly complex in our minds. Our journey is from bondage, isolation and loneliness to reconciliation, reunion, communion and grace. All the trials we must face are opportunities to peer through the veil of illusion and to make contact with that which we truly want.

This is the life we live. If we can be innocently open to our longing, the entire experience of being alive will be different. It's all a matter of recovering the innocence of our longing heart. It's childlike, simple, and always there. And it's enormously vulnerable.

Where does that take you, Lisa?

Lisa: I just want to ask Terri if she felt a breakthrough in her resistance. It felt that way to me.

Terri: Yes.

Lisa: You broke through the barrier to that vulnerable part of yourself.

Lisa, if you were able to see yourself for a moment, to hear you, to feel you, to experience who you are through eyes that haven't been sullied by shame, through a kind of angelic innocence, you would see a person who is deep, soft and enormously sensitive. You wouldn't resemble the kind of person that you perceive yourself to be. There is nothing in the outward sphere that you could accomplish; there isn't any success you could have in terms of the world that would compensate for missing this view of yourself.

Lisa: As you speak, I'm wanting to put myself in your position, to see myself like you see me.

Yes, because what you experience so much of the time is a kind of strangulation, a struggle, like there's something tied around you.

Lisa: Yes.

And you are saying you would love to be able to experience yourself without that strangulation, without that tightness. Let's go to the body. What do you experience now as you sit with the body? What is your feeling experience?

Lisa: I feel a lot of vibration.

Everywhere in your body?

Lisa: Maybe in my heart.

Let's go to the vibration. Can you be with it very directly? Let's just be with it for a minute or two....Now also allow your attention to be with me, gently, softly. Do you feel alone, Lisa? Is the struggle a dominant force right now, or is there something softer, more open and more available?

Lisa: I feel that I'm blending with the vibrations from my heart to your heart.

I feel that too. And that's real, yes? That's not an idea. That's an experience you're having.

Lisa: I can only think of your own words, that there is no space between us.

Let's be with each other for a few minutes. Do you feel some love in the body, some warmth?

Lisa: Yes.

Is there a struggle around that love, Lisa?

Lisa: Yes, there is a struggle.

And can you identify what that struggle might be? What is your sense of what you are trying to get away from by not accepting this love fully?

Lisa: What comes to mind is my whole issue with my daughter, when she attacks me and blames me for her unhappiness. Then I take it in and I feel her woundedness and my woundedness as one. But somehow I'm not able to get beyond it — that sense that something's wrong with me and that it has caused something to be wrong with her. It's an infection in relationship. What is it?

How does that relate to your present experience?

Lisa: It's like a shadow.

But when you spoke of your daughter in the context of what you're feeling now, did you do that because there was some experience of hurt that came up for you and you went to your memory to explain it?

Lisa: I don't know why I went to her. I think that when you asked about what the struggle was....it's a mental thing, a struggle between the human and the divine.

But Lisa, where are you right this minute? My experience of you is that you are in a struggle and that the struggle is a twisting away from an encounter. Do you follow what I'm saying?

Lisa: Yes, I do.

We were, for a moment, having an encounter with one another, and then you started moving into an arena that was tight. You started to pull away from the meeting we were having.

Lisa: Yes, I want to erase that.

But maybe it's more useful just to look at it for a moment and to see that at a subtle physical level you were attempting to tighten yourself up so much that you weren't available anymore. It is as if, for a moment, there was an opening and then an attempt to make yourself thinner, smaller, more contracted, less physical, less available.

Lisa: Yes, yes.

And all that happened through fantasy, speculation, insight, remembering something that occurred once. On the surface it looked like you were trying to make sense out of what was happening, but you were actually pulling away from relationship.

Now let's come back to this moment together, where we are now and experience whatever is here.... I can feel you again. You were actually trying to disappear. You understand what I'm saying?

Lisa: I do.

Disappearing by becoming more dense, thinner, out of spaciousness into contraction, into the head and away from the connecting point. That's a reflex. We are looking at a reflex in relationship to relationship, in relationship to what we would call energetic intimacy, love. But the word strangulation is important here. Do you know what I mean?

Lisa: Oh my, yes.

The word strangulated in terms of the way you struggle with your desire and your capacity to accept, to give love. Let's go back to the heart, back to the body. Do you feel me, Lisa. Do you love me?

Lisa: Yes.

And do you know that I love you?

Lisa: Yes.

You can feel that?

Lisa: Yes.

Let's feel that together. Is there anything else that truly matters?

Lisa: No.

Let's sit together for a moment now. There is a change in the quality of light a person radiates as they open to love. When a person contracts, something actually disappears. You can't find them anymore. A kind of blackness emerges. As a person rests into love, allowing it to be felt in the body, then the black lightens, turns bluish and then can transform in a golden light. That is you. Our surface perceptions of this life are just the dimmest reflection of a beautiful artistic process which is occurring at levels we aren't allowing ourselves to experience.

You are not only Lisa, with her memories and personality; that's only the faintest aspect of who you are; that's only the thread of an illusion. You are an incandescence, an illumination. And when you try to escape from love by contracting the body, the radiance dims and diminishes somewhat.

There are people who actually flicker. They are present for a moment, related, then they are gone. It can be frustrating to connect with people who do this because they constantly offer a taste of something, but as soon as it becomes available and felt by another, it is withdrawn. It's a constant loss. It is self-consciousness which gives rise to those contractions. As self-consciousness disappears, radiance arises and as self-consciousness appears, radiance diminishes.

Do you follow me?

Lisa: Yes.

It's like a digestive problem. Only so much love can be absorbed at once. There is a fear about taking too much in. You take in a certain amount, then you hold it and try to get more. But as you hold it, a struggle is created and you are no longer available to yourself or to someone else.

You are a pulsation, a vibrating radiance which has certain tones and qualities that are unique to your body. When a person comes into an experience with you, especially if there is an openness, then they can feel you. They love you and are attracted to you. When you contract and hold back, then that openness is not there. No one is being fed. There is frustration and maybe the desire to attack.

Jon: Steve, I just got what you're describing now. I am so aware of that. I could feel Lisa disappearing when she began to talk about her relationship between her daughter and herself. And when you raised the issue of her in relationship to you, that's where I came alive and could feel all that stuff. But the question that comes to me is that when we're engaged in the energetic realm and we're feeling the dialogue, the back and forthness of energies between us, that's alive for me. I don't get that experience with the other stuff you spoke of earlier.

But I'm not clear why that matters so much.

Jon: It matters because you spent an hour on it and I felt sleepier and sleepier. And so my mind comes in and says, "Well, Jon, you're not really understanding this." It matters because I think there's something I'm not getting or understanding and so I raise the question.

You could follow your experience without tying a knot in it so that it can emerge into consciousness in a different way. Maybe falling asleep has nothing to do with not getting something, maybe it represents a part of yourself which is getting out of the way so that this other experience of aliveness can begin to come forth. Maybe you should follow the sleepiness, stay with it, allow it and see what arises on the other side — as opposed to stopping it somewhere and trying to get an insight about it.

When I speak like I did for an hour or so, I'm paving the way. What happens in this circle is not casual. What happens here usually doesn't occur in our ordinary social affairs. We don't often experience each other as radiant energies. My talks are a kind of preparation for a different way of relating to ourselves. Some people get angry, some bored, others are totally enlivened by it, moved deeply. To me it doesn't matter at all.

There is some element of knotting, of frustration, that I feel from you in terms of this. You let yourself slide just so far and then you put a knot in it. You try to stop the movement. The knot is a kind of judgment or introspection that becomes an obstacle to a full experience. There is anger in it, Jon. That anger is the result of putting a surgical band around a flow, constricting it. Do you know what I'm saying?

You constrict yourself in a certain way and it expresses as anger. This happens because you won't let something develop in an organic way. You close it off with a judgment.

First there is a movement, then a hardening, a tightening. An experience occurs which forces you into a congested position until an explosion comes. The task you face involves allowing an experience to occur instead of making a judgment about it and then stopping it.

Many people feel energetic congestion, a knot. People who experience this are often attracted to cathartic experiences because it gives them the chance to explode. The explosion feels like a release. It feels good. It looks like progress is being made on a deep level.

The spiritual path is not a series of cathartic experiences. It is a movement toward deep trust and a patient, attentive waiting for the tightness to unfurl itself. We do not aim for catharsis, breakthrough or release in some dramatic way, but rather toward an experience of complete self-respect in which it is recognized that everything we feel is innocent and holy, everything we feel is energy.

Energetic congestion, which is translated by the mind into emotional difficulty, comes as a result of tightening against a flow. Cooperation is a process in which experience is allowed to unfold. It is not forced, coerced or pushed into a mold. Every one of us is dealing with our own relationship to cosmic energy. No one is exempt. All our problems are equal. Some are simply more dramatic than others.

When we discuss the internal knot, the running away from relationship, disappearing and energetic flickering, we are not exploring personal failure or neurosis, but rather an evolutionary process of which we are all a part. Whatever way our particular holdback manifests is our task, our individual work. Our journey can not be compared to someone else's. It's not fair. Comparisons like that are a distraction from what is important, from the work at hand.

Our personal obstacles represent evolutionary friction. It is necessary and dignified to work with that friction in such a way that we find the strength and dignity which lie just behind the judgment. Getting rid of the friction by seeking peace through catharsis or insight is not the way.

Our life is a process of digestion. We are being fed all the time. We are constantly engaged in the transmutation of one substance into another. Energies are received, changed and given back in an altered form. Spiritual work is a process in which a human being learns to digest the energy of love more completely.

Some people feel heavy all the time, full; some people feel hungry, empty or starved, never able to get enough; some people find life irritating and others feel dull or sleepy much of the time. Some feel nausea. These experiences represent our particular relationship to the life force as it enters into our form. The task is to clarify, cooperate and gently assist a much greater process than our personal concerns.

Lucy: May I say something to Jon? When he was talking about his sleepiness, that sounded to me like an automatic kindness of his own, that he can hear when he's asleep. He can hear clearly when he's asleep. Or maybe it's not really sleep; maybe he can hear it there too. I'm sure of it.

I'm sure of it too. What you are saying is precise. I don't know how Jon hears it, but I can relate to what you're saying.

Lucy: I had to say it, not that he has to accept it or agree with it.

How do you take that in Jon?

Jon: Well, I'm not sure that I heard it all, that when I'm asleep....

Could I interrupt you for a moment, because this is the whole process here. Maybe before you start your response to Lucy, you could just sense where you're coming from in talking to her? Where do you feel yourself? How do you experience yourself right now?

Jon: Well, on one level, I feel close to her. I feel warmed by her being here, by her addressing me, by her interest in saying the things that she said. And then there's another level, the level of the concepts and ideas. I didn't hear it all. A part of me wants to be clear about the thoughts she is expressing.

Is there a way for those two things to meet?

Jon: That's a good question. If there were, I could leave now. I'd have it all.

Let's go to the body for a moment and maybe you could express what you're feeling.

Jon: Excitement, joy, love.

And those are distinctly physical?

Jon: Oh, yes.

Can you say something to Lucy from that place?

Jon: If I could do that, then my wife and I would get along so well.

Can you do it though, is it here?

Jon: God, I'm caught in the act here. Well....this is a real education. It's really interesting how hard it is for me to do that, and yet it's right there.

Is it all right if I add something? I don't want to interrupt your process but there's something important here. When you initially started to speak in response to Lucy, your tone could have been interpreted as combative.

Jon: Really?

As coming out of a kind of aggression. Then when I said come back to the body, all of that left. There was a split between the conceptual and the knowingness, the conceptual and the body. Your response was almost like a separate force, tight and unrelated to a greater organic process. And then when we came back to the body, something became integrated. There was room for some expression to Lucy on an entirely different level. One could feel, and I'm not saying this was felt, but especially given the delicacy of what Lucy said, a slight shiver of tension in regard to the way you spoke with her. But in this space, there wouldn't be any combativeness, even if the very same question were asked.

Jon: It really does call for an opening to a dimension that gets split off.

Where do you feel yourself right now?

Jon: Well, I'm in a struggle to allow that dimension to be there, to come from there in the things I say.

Can you characterize the struggle at a slightly less symbolic level? In other words, how do you feel that struggle?

Jon: There are the relationship energies that I feel. And that seems so subtle and unimportant, although I know that sounds weird. It's like a small corner of something much bigger. I want to get this intellectually. That seems like the real stuff and this other stuff seems so unimportant, although I'm sure that's not the case.

What do you want right now?

Jon: Well, I sure want your intervention because it brings me up short and shows me my resistance to the energy.

What do you feel towards Lucy? Is there a tone, a feeling experience?

Jon: Yes, I feel a connection. I feel tears coming when you ask me that. I'm very moved and touched by it all.

Can you just stay with that, give it complete permission to be there? Is there some quality in your feelings right now that you might be willing to express? Is it like love, some softness toward her or toward anyone here?

Jon: Oh, yes.

Can you say something directly to Lucy?

Jon: You're putting me on the spot, but I love it.... I feel love for you, Lucy, and I just feel myself holding back and not wanting to say that. It's embarrassing.

Lucy: Thank you, Jon.

Now stay with the body, Jon. Can you see the relationship between something in you going to sleep, something in you having to go away before you can take all this in?

Jon: Yeah, I mean I went to sleep because I was trying to take in what you were saying with my mind.

Yes, and it couldn't handle it in that sense.

Jon: No, it sure couldn't.

Let's stay with the body now Jon, just stay with the body.

Jon: I feel a lot of excitement and joy and softness, and a connectedness with you and with everybody here.

And as you're sitting here in that experience, does it feel tight or constricted in any way?

Jon: I can feel something on the outside that wants to encircle it somehow.

Can you identify that? Can you characterize it a little more concretely perhaps?

Jon: That encirclement is the way to survive in life. That's the way to live, presumably.

The encirclement is a belief structure?

Jon: Yes.

This is an important observation and it comes out of being in a quiet space. The encirclement is like a downward pressure and the love is an ascending force, however soft. They both sit together. When the attention is shifted to the body and content is dropped, even briefly, the ascending force can be experienced more directly and the downward pressure is diminished somewhat. The downward force is thought, beliefs and ideas, however unconscious, and the body's response to those beliefs. The ascending force is something else.

Jon: I didn't even know there was a belief structure. I just felt the encirclement, but it is a belief. I have to be tight in order to survive.

That is a fundamental statement: I must sacrifice my love and my self-expression in order to survive. We can carry beliefs like that for a long time. We end up constructing our life in such a way that it appears to affirm the belief and many of the choices we make are in accordance with it, but in the background we long for something else.

Jon: I've not been aware of the hunger as much as other people seem to be.

I think you are aware of the hunger, not so much as a longing of the heart, but as the need to know something.

Jon: Right, right.

A piece of you gets broken off from the whole and when this occurs a certain aggression arises, an intellectual aggression, if you will. This aggression appears like the need to understand on a conceptual level. It becomes a distracted channeling of your longing. When you come back to the body, then the longing can be experienced more directly.

Jon: Wow!

There is a modality of defense in your relationship to love or life-current. It doesn't matter what words we use. A part of you breaks off and misinterprets your longing as a hunt for knowledge. Your personal task has nothing to do with getting over this or becoming like someone else, but rather to integrate the intellectual capacity with that something else, so that the longing and the intellectual capacity can be as one.

Jon: My guess is that this is true for men in general.

Maybe, but it is important to understand the individual nature of your task.

Jon: Yes.

You could see certain circumstances emerging in your life as a way to practice reunion and reconciliation and not an opportunity to divorce yourself from the deeper side. A circumstance arises in your life and your reflex might be divorce — to break the intellect from the body. There is a choice however in such circumstances. We can gently begin to practice returning our attention to the heart and staying steady with that.

This is how we cooperate with our evolutionary task. We respectfully acknowledge one reflex and then choose a free act instead. We choose to be with ourselves as a whole instead of breaking off. Healing is a process of organic reconciliation. The problem is synthetic and fragmented.

Jon: I feel such gratitude now for your having stopped me and for your help here. I'm so moved, and it feels so big.

I can experience you now as a man who has united the intellectual level with the feeling level. A kind of greatness has emerged. Gratitude and humility are a natural outcome of being in touch with the greatness of our own gift. It is not ours. Gratitude is not a trivial experience.

Your gift is related to your capacity to unite the sense of awe, which is generated at the intellectual level, with the feeling of wonder and humility at the bodily level. It is a beautiful gift.

Jon: I feel so much awe I can't even talk anymore. Thank you, Stephen.

Other Books By Stephen Schwartz

Visualization: Breaking Through the Illusion of Problems

Problems Are the Doors Through Which We Walk to Peace

The Compassionate Presence: Meeting and Greeting a Love that Will Not End

Prayer of the Body

I Accept in All Gratitude: Cancer, Crisis and Compassionate Self-Care

For more information on books and recordings, and further writings of
STEPHEN ROBBINS SCHWARTZ
please see the website:
compassionateselfcare.wordpress.com
or contact his widow, Donna, at
dtotten@whidbey.com